THE LIFE OF

A TEENAGE GIRL

Stories About Finding Your Way

By

Kukua Appiah

Published by Truth Communications Media & Publications

Printed in Canada

ISBN 978-1-998935-04-8

Dedication

I give thanks to God for giving me the chance to create these lovely stories. Without His grace and mercy, I don't think I would have ever found this passion for writing.

I also want to thank my publisher, Wayne Hinds, and the fantastic team at Truth Communications for believing in my story even when it was barely seen or heard. Your support made me feel noticed, encouraged, and confident in my ideas.

Finally, I want to say a big thank you to my mom. Without her support, prayers, and encouragement, I wouldn't have had the confidence to share my writing. Thank you, Mom, for being there for me, even on the days when planning felt hard.

TABLE OF CONTENTS

THAT WASN'T THE PLAN

"A best friend's love, or a boyfriend's love?"

CHAPTER 1

My older sister woke me up early at 7:00 a.m. She opened the curtains, letting out a bright, yellow, and orange light from the sun. It was going to be a normal school day, but this morning made me feel like it was going to be different.

"Ugh, Myra, why'd you wake me up?" I groaned, squinting my eyes from the light outside.

"Because we have to go to school, and I always have to be forced to come here and wake you up," Myra said.

I had no choice. If I kept lying on the bed for long, I knew my sister would go to my Mom and snitch on me. And then my Mom would barge into my room with an angry or annoyed frown and scold me for not doing what I'm supposed to do. This is literally how life is in my family. My Mom can be a worry, my Dad is kind of a boring guy, my sister always acts like an annoying complainer, and I, the positive overthinker, easily fall for things. I feel like my family and I inherited these personalities from our past ancestors and family members. If that even makes sense.

Anyway, I got ready for school in my new outfit for the day. A light–blue baggy jeans with a common white shirt. My Dad wanted to do my hair for the school week because he thinks he doesn't do anything much for me anymore. So yesterday, he French braided my hair, leaving messy leftover parts on top of my head and curly bangs in front of my face. To be honest, I kind of liked it, even though it was a bit messy and he didn't really do the braids well. I still appreciated it.

I went downstairs and saw my Mom cleaning the wooden dinner table. I sat beside Myra, took a slice of bread, and put PB on it.

"Mom, no need to drive me today, I'm walking with Jayson."

My Mom finally finished cleaning my side of the table.

"Are you sure? What if he doesn't come, or doesn't want to walk?"

That actually made sense, but I know my best friend likes walking, and his parents barely have time to drive or take him to school. Besides, we always walk wherever we want to go. He *has* to walk with me to school today.

But sometimes he ditches me, though.

I took a bite of my PB bread, "Don't worry, Mum, I'm sure he's going to come by the door, and knock in 5… 4… 3…"

I turned to the door, waiting and hoping Jayson was probably walking to the porch, and…

"—2…1," A knock and a familiar voice were heard; everyone already knew it was Jayson.

I walked to the door quickly, wearing my black Converse, and opened the door.

"Hey, Jay," I waved.

Jayson smiled and looked inside to greet my Mom.

"Uh, goodbye, Mrs. Sanchez."

My Mom waved at him, and I pulled him out, and we walked down the street.

Jayson and I have been good friends—well, not just friends, *best friends* —since we were kids. Our parents met at a night festival, and when they brought us together, we connected like magnets. We even kept the same old photo of us from years ago, tucked into our wallets. It became our quiet pact. If either of us ever threw it away, it would mean the friendship was over. But neither Jayson nor I have ever done that. And we never will.

"So," I cleared my throat. "What happened back in Italy? Did you have a good weekend?"

Jayson gripped his backpack tightly, "Yeah. I stayed with my cousins and Nonna."

"Your Nonna? Oh, I love her! Even though I met her once, she's still the best grandma I've ever talked to," I shrieked in happiness.

He then stopped and took something from his bag, like a small brown box. "Well, she misses you, so she told me to give you some of her new, fresh bomboloni desserts,"

"Oh my gosh! Really?" I covered my mouth in surprise.

He handed the small box of bomboloni dessert to me, "Yeah, and it's filled with your favorites, jam, cream, and Nutella."

I opened the box, smelling the goodness and delight of the desserts.

"Aw, please tell her I said thank you."

Jayson smiled and nodded.

CHAPTER 2

Parkland High was where we attended school. Jayson and I went to our lockers, which were at the far end of the school building. It was a long hallway since the school was big, and we had to walk about five minutes, our legs shaking and wobbly because of the distance. But we'd done this before—since we started at the school.

And sometimes, I'd beg Jayson to carry me to our lockers or even to our classes. He's done it once before—which was a year ago.

When we finally made it to our lockers—mine was always beside his—we had the same photo on each locker to prove we were best friends. That was the pact, and no one could separate us.

Nellie walked over with someone new—a guy with curly brown hair, a plain white shirt, and khaki shorts. I caught myself staring longer than I should've, tracing from his hazel eyes down to the way he carried himself.

In my head, I was already spiraling.

Maybe this is it. Maybe this week is finally the start of my boyfriend plan.

I started thinking about all the things I could list—what it takes to be a girlfriend, how to actually get a boyfriend, and the kind of guy I was hoping he'd be. I know that was kind of random, but I had to.

I immediately snapped out of it, took out my books for the first two classes, and turned back to my friends.

"Hey, Nellie," I waved, looking at both her and the guy.

Nellie placed her arm around the guy's shoulder, smiling. "Hey, guys, this is Chris. He's the new student here—and my new friend."

I turned to Jayson, and he looked at me. We gave each other an *Oh really* look.

You see, Nellie is a cool, sweet girl. She's the type of person who loves to chit–chat about things—mostly to gossip, though—and she has a bunch of friends because of that.

But anytime a new person comes to her neighborhood, school, or just anywhere she's in, she, of course, gossips about them. She normally doesn't bother to look, talk, or even be nice to the new person. And all her friends came to her and befriended her first. So, her saying he's her new friend kinda sounds weird—and doesn't make sense. Unless Chris went to her first.

Anyway, Jayson and I turned back to Nellie and the guy. I stared right at Chris first.

"I'm Kandis. Nice to meet you."

Chris extended his hand to mine, and I shook it gently.
"Nice name, Kandis."

But when I shook his hand, it felt so warm. He squeezed my hand, and for some reason, I didn't complain or pull away.

He then turned to Jayson, who had a *'I don't think I like this guy'* look.

Chris also brought his hand to him. "You must be...?"

"Jayson. But sorry, I don't like shaking people's hands."

That felt like a lie. Jayson *does* like shaking people's hands. He always extends his hand to people he's just met. Even if he's known them for a long time, he still likes to shake hands. It's his way of being polite—and that's something I like about him.

"Oh, well, it's good to meet you both anyway." Chris forced a smile and slowly put his hand away.

CHAPTER 3

In History class, I was sitting in the middle with Jayson, since he was my partner for most classes. Anytime we were in the same class, I'd always be his partner—whether for projects or assignments.

Our substitute, Mrs. Hardwood, said we should just work on our last project before the weekend started. It was a two-partner project about the study of historical figures.

I turned to Jayson, who was taking out the long white construction paper we were going to do our project on.

"So, what historical figure are we doing?"

Jayson opened his laptop, searching for a figure. "Hmm... maybe William Shakespeare?"

"The English playwright, poet, and actor?" I tilted my head. "I thought you didn't like English people."

He chuckled under his breath. "Yeah, but he writes the best stories that I like."

"What type of stories?" I glanced at his face.

Jayson leaned in, lowering his voice like a whisper. "*Romeo and Juliet.* You know, like... romance."

I was a bit confused when he leaned so close to my face. I could already feel his breath on my skin. Well, I mean, Jayson can be an over-friendly, *so-close-to-loving* type anyway. His actions can seem like more than friendship—but he's my best friend. He sometimes does this to lift my mood if I'm sad or upset, or just to get on my nerves.

"Romance, really?" I blinked rapidly, slowly pulling back. "I should've known."

"What can I say, Kandis? I can be a book nerd sometimes." He shrugged and leaned back in his seat.

After getting through History and Science, lunch finally came. I walked into the cafeteria and headed straight to my usual spot—back middle, same table, same friends.

I pulled out my veggie sandwich and tea just as Chris slid into the seat beside me. He looked at me with that soft expression—the kind that made it impossible to know what he was thinking.

"I see you're a vegetarian," he smiled.

I nodded with pleasure. "Yeah. Are you too?"

"No, but I support people who are."

Chris leaned against my arm, his hand brushing mine. I felt butterflies in my stomach. My face turned light pink as he took one slice of my tomato, ate it, and winked at me.

It seemed Jayson saw it too—and was angry about it. He clenched his fists on the table with a loud thump, which made Chris sit up straight in his chair.

CHAPTER 4

After school ended, I walked with Jayson to our neighbourhood. Normally, Nellie also walks with us, but since her parents got a new car last month, she's been getting *princess–car* treatment—which means car rides home every day. In a Mercedes–Benz.

Sometimes I wonder if she actually wants to walk home with us as friends, or if she'd rather sit in a luxury car and drive home, relaxing in it. Even though walking is way worse than driving, sometimes it can be fun and have good reasons—like exercising your body by running or jogging, having a quiet moment to yourself, or just exploring the town around you.

But I don't think Nellie would care about that, because she literally has everything she needs at home. So, I kind of understand why she wouldn't want to walk back with us.

Anyway, Jayson and I reached our street, and since we live next to each other, it didn't take long for us to get home at the same time.

I heard some voices in the kitchen and went to check it out. It was my Uncle Eddie talking to my mom, and I was really happy—and surprised—to see him. Uncle Eddie has been in our hometown, Australia, for as long as I can remember. The last time I saw him was when I was ten, and now I'm fifteen. He was the only one in my family who made me feel like myself sometimes.

"Uncle Eddie!" I ran to him, kind of interrupting his conversation with my mom.

I realized I actually was, because Mom suddenly gave me a troubled look.

Uncle Eddie turned to me, opening his arms wide. "Ohh, my favourite niece!"

But I didn't care—I hugged him as tightly as I could. "I missed you so much!"

"Me too. I mostly came here to see and visit you. And gosh, you've grown so big, Kandis!"

He pulled back from the hug, though I still kept my hands around him. "How long are you staying here this time?"

"Oh, Kandis, you know I visit for about three days when I come by—it's the same this time too!"

I groaned. I really didn't want him to stay that short. Whenever Uncle Eddie is here, it's always good times. He usually takes Myra and me to Six Flags, big cities, or even car trips to, like… the woods! I could never regret having him as my uncle.

"But three days isn't enough—at least half a week?" I begged him.

"Sorry, Kandis, but no can do." He shook his head slowly. "I've got a lot of business work to catch up on—and with your dad too. That's another reason I came. But don't worry, we're still going to have fun!"

I sighed and agreed. I could totally understand Dad and Uncle Eddie having serious work to do. Dad is always working anyway, and he sometimes asks Uncle Eddie to help. That's even why I can say

Uncle Eddie is better than Dad—because Dad barely gets time to have fun with me.

CHAPTER 5

A nyway, I talked with Uncle Eddie for a bit, and after eating my dinner, I walked upstairs to my room to start making my plan.

The *"get a boyfriend this year"* plan.

Because this year—this tenth–grade semester—I really wanted to date someone. I've had thousands of people I've had feelings for, but they were never *the one.* So, one by one, I listed some things and qualities I wanted my boyfriend to have:

1. Has to be the same age as me or just one year older.
2. Needs to be a good guy—maybe funny, but of course, loyal.
3. Needs to accept that I can sometimes be shy or weird.
4. Has to accept my friends, especially my best friend.

So far, these were the only four things I could think of. But I didn't really think they were enough, because, as a human, you need at least five or more personality traits to be a love partner (in my opinion).

So, I called Jayson to try to help me.

He answered in five seconds. "Hey, Kandis."

I turned it into a video call so he could see the list I made.

"Hey, asleep yet?"

He shook his head and rubbed his hair. "No, what do you need?"

"So, this year, I've decided—maybe I should try getting a... partner. You know, since tenth grade is full of romance and not even learning."

Jayson paused, staring right into the screen. Then he folded his lips and cleared his throat. "Um... you mean, like a boyfriend?"

"Yeah, and I've even made a list of qualities and things I want my boyfriend to be."

I started reading the things I'd written on the list to him, and after about three seconds, he stopped me mid–sentence.

"Okay, Kandis..." His voice sounded like he was in pain. "I—I don't really think it's a good idea to do this."

"Why? I thought you even said you wanted a girlfriend when you turned fourteen?"

"Yeah, but... that was two years ago, and I'm sixteen now, not fourteen. Shouldn't we be focusing on other important stuff?"

"Like what? School subjects? Our *future career*? Oh, please, Jayson! Once in our lives, we need to find our soulmate."

"Well, I don't want to! I feel like I'm not ready, Kandis."

I slowly put the list away, giving him all my attention, because I really wanted to understand what he meant. Since ninth grade ended for him two years ago, his first wish was to get a love partner—even before senior year. But now, I'm bringing it up and asking to get a boyfriend, and he's somehow annoyed by it?

"Jay?" My voice softened. "Are you being serious right now? One day you're talking about something you really want, and the next day you want to forget it. What's going on?"

"Nothing. I'm just not feeling it today. I'm not feeling like getting a *girlfriend*." He shrugged nonchalantly and made air quotes around the word *girlfriend*.

I wanted to say something to defend my plan, but he stopped me and said he wanted to go to bed. Even though, when I checked my phone clock, it was just 7:30 p.m.—and we usually sleep at the same time, 9 p.m.

So it was like he was finding an excuse not to talk about the plan anymore.

He waved through the screen and clicked the hang–up button right before I said goodnight.

CHAPTER 6

The next day at school, I had Literacy class first thing in the morning—and surprisingly, Chris had it too. I didn't know any other friends in the class, and the people there weren't really the type I liked to talk to or chat with. Well, except Samara, the class president—but she wasn't even there.

Anyway, I sat in the back with Chris, who was beside me. Like, literally a desk beside me. I could feel his arm pressed against mine. I think he did that to get my attention.

After Mr. San Diego finished teaching us the lesson units, he assigned us to work on the questions in our textbook and told us to ask our desk partner for help if needed. And Chris gave himself a chance to talk to me—like he actually needed help.

"So… Kandis." He stared right at me, making me shiver a bit. "I kind of need help, and I hear you're good at Literacy."

I swallowed hard; my feelings were making me hesitate. "Uh… yeah, I am. What do you need help with?"

"This question." He dragged his hand to the book.

I wrote the question in my notebook, then explained it with lots of details and information from the textbook. But I already knew he understood it—because from his face, he knew the answer. He was just finding an excuse to talk to me. Which, of course, I didn't hate. I actually liked it.

After we finished answering the questions, we put our books away, and I decided to bring out my plan from last night. Even though Jayson annoyed me by not helping with it, I barely cared anymore—because I figured I could work on it myself anyway.

I started writing some benefits and qualities of being a girlfriend and left the *boyfriend* part aside. But luckily for me, Chris actually saw what I was doing and wanted to know what it was about.

"What are you doing, Kandis?"

I paused while writing the fourth quality. "Oh, this year, I'm planning on trying to get a boyfriend, and right now I'm thinking about the things I want my boyfriend to be—and how I can be a girlfriend."

"Wow, that's… that's cool, I guess. So far, only four?" He raised his eyebrows, looking surprised.

"Yeah, it's not really going well. I can't find much to write about."

Chris scratched his head, thinking for a moment. "Um… maybe I could help?"

I was a bit stunned that he wanted to help. I mean—why did he want to? Why did he care? Why did he bother? I'd only told him half of what I was planning, and he was already interested and wanted to help. But I didn't resist (like Jayson did) and allowed him to help.

So, he took the list and started writing tips and little things I might need in a boyfriend. He even helped by giving me ideas on how to be a girlfriend. I was astonished.

"Wow, Chris. This is great—so sweet of you."

He handed the list back to me. "No bother. You'll probably get a boyfriend before this week ends, I'm sure."

I was already feeling butterflies in my stomach. The way he said I'd get a boyfriend this week made me feel like it was going to be him. I mean, this *has* to be a connection, right? Because then why would he even give me tips and ideas? This is a total clue.

CHAPTER 7

Noon hit, and it was lunchtime. I went to the cafeteria to meet my friends at our table in the back, but only Nellie and Chris were there. Jayson was late—and he's never late. He and I usually come to the table at the same time. But I still waited for him while talking to Nellie and Chris.

"Okay, guys, I'm here," said Jayson, approaching us and sitting beside Nellie.

I took out my lunch and slipped into the seat next to Jayson, but he acted like he didn't see or notice me and turned to face Nellie and Chris.

At that point, I was confused. First, he made me angry last night about my plan, then he didn't walk or talk to me the whole morning, and now he was ignoring everything I did. Something was definitely going on—either he was upset about something or he was just being a nuisance.

"Jay," I tried to get his attention.

He turned to me slowly, trying to take his eyes away from my face. "Yeah?"

I couldn't even say anything. It was like he didn't even want to talk to me in any way. He realized I was quiet and went back to chatting with Nellie and Chris.

After fifteen minutes in the cafeteria, I finished my lunch and got saved by the bell. It wasn't that lunch was over, but anytime the clock hit 12:15, most of the guys in the room had to go to the gym for soccer practice. Luckily, Chris and Jayson both played soccer, so they left, leaving me and Nellie at the table.

It was my chance to ask Nellie about Jayson's behavior—and why he was acting so irritated toward me.

"Hey, Nellie, I need to ask you something."

She packed her lunch and placed it into her bag. "Yeah?"

"Do you know why Jayson is acting so… weird?"

"What do you mean?"

I sighed softly. "Like, he's acting different around me—ever since last night when we called."

"Last night? Different? Kandis, I don't know what you're talking about. He seems normal." She shrugged like nothing was going on.

"Well, not to me. He's totally changed."

"Okay, I guess I can understand." She put her hand on her chin, lost in another thought. "Because before lunch, when we were having our Literacy class, I was there. And I guess you didn't know, because I actually saw you and Chris talking to each other in an… unusual way."

I raised my eyebrows, stunned. I definitely didn't know or realize Nellie also had the Literacy class. I should've checked my schedule, but… why did it bother me so much? I mean, why did it matter that she was there, watching me and Chris talk about relationships and all?

"And…" Nellie brought me back to reality. "When I asked for the bathroom access, I saw Jayson at his locker on my way back. I went to say hi, and he asked me how class was going."

She then paused, swallowing her words.

"Okay, what happened after?" I rushed her.

Nellie blinked as her long eyelashes curled up. "I told him what we were doing in Literacy class—and also what you were doing with Chris. But he didn't seem a bit happy about it. I mean, I don't know, he just frowned, slammed his locker, and left."

I pulled back into the seat, furrowing my eyebrows in confusion. Why would he be upset about that? Jayson barely cared about my feelings for boys or even talking to them. He used to take videos of me crushing and having a meltdown whenever my crushes talked to me and told me he'd show them to me when I grew up, and I'd just cringe. I knew it was a joke—we were very young, and we didn't care. He still has those videos, but now… he acts so weird when I'm around boys.

CHAPTER 8

I went straight home without talking or hanging out with any of my friends. I actually wanted to find out where Jayson was since he'd left the cafeteria for soccer practice, and we didn't talk or see each other again. Even when school ended, I already knew he had gone home because, of course, he didn't wait for me.

So I stopped. I decided to just stop trying to talk to him. If he wouldn't tell me what was going on—fine. If he kept getting annoyed that I was talking about boyfriends and hanging out with Chris—fine. I was fed up with him anyway.

I reached home later, at 3:10, and went straight to my room. I took out the boyfriend plan and laid it on my bed. But I immediately thought of today—at school and even last night when Jayson and I talked. I thought of Chris when he helped write more qualities. And for some reason, I didn't feel like finishing it. I didn't feel like getting a boyfriend anymore. And it was a 75% feeling.

Uncle Eddie was still home, and since it was only me, him, and Myra who were available for the rest of the day, we decided to go to the city and hang out for a bit—just for the last time we'd see Uncle before Saturday. We came back home around 3:30.

Anyway, in my room, after I finished undressing and working on my school project, I got a call—and it was from Chris. I wondered why he'd be calling me; no boy had ever called me. Unless Jayson, but forget him—he'd made me mad.

"Um, hi, Chris," I answered the call.

Chris cleared his throat softly. "Hey, I'm glad you picked up."

"Yeah, how'd you get my number?"

"Nellie. She gave it to me."

I nodded, looking anywhere but the phone. "Oh. Why'd you call?"

Chris stammered, pausing in his sentences. "Um… I wanted to— to ask you something. I hope you would… say yes."

"Say yes to what?" My voice went low and soft—it sounded like a low-pitched, weird voice. But I was actually thinking he wanted to ask me something related to the boyfriend list I made, and maybe he wanted more of that.

"Well, I know we've only been friends for about two days and talked for a while, but I wanted to know if you would want to hang out with me somewhere," Chris said.

I raised my eyebrows. This truly meant something—something significant. What Chris was trying to say was that he liked me. More than a friend! And that he wanted to hang out with me.

"Oh, Chris, that's lovely. Of course, I'd want to hang out with you."

He chuckled lightly through the screen, and for a second, it felt like he was smiling just for me. "Really? Great, glad you said yes. I was thinking of that new big park that opened last week."

"Sure, seems cool. When?"

"Tomorrow, Saturday night."

"Like… a date?"

I honestly don't know why I said that. I think I just assumed he meant hanging out like a Saturday night date kind of thing. It sounded like that to me. And like I said—I'm pretty sure he likes me. But still, I kind of regretted asking if it was a "date."

"Well, no—not really. Unless that's what you want. I mean, I thought it could be like a friend hangout, since we just started talking less than a week ago," he answered.

I totally agreed, though. "Of course. A friend's hangout is fine."

"Great. I'll meet you in the park around 6 p.m. See you there."

I waved goodbye, and he ended the call.

I was so happy this was happening—it was my first time going out with a boy, and I couldn't believe it! I wanted to tell Jayson about it and how happy I was, but… because of the silent argument we'd been having all week, I didn't feel like telling him. Just like at school, when he found out about me and Chris, he'd be upset.

CHAPTER 9

The next day was going to be special. I got up and got ready for my hangout. I went to my closet and picked out the outfit I was going to wear. It was a short, denim, box-pleat skirt and a white tube top with a black sweater. I was even going to wear my new black and white Jordans.

Then suddenly, my door opened, and my sister entered, eating brown toast with a cup of orange juice in her hand.

"What are you doing here?" I asked, putting the clothes on my hook rack.

"Just checking to see if you were up. It's now my job to wake you up anytime you're sleeping in," Myra said, taking a bite of her toast.

"Whatever. As you can see, I'm awake, so get out."

"Firstly, Mum told me to call you downstairs for breakfast, and secondly, what're you doing?"

I rolled my eyes and closed the door behind her. "I'm doing an outfit check for a friend hangout tonight."

"Ooh, a friend hangout? Tonight?" She pouted her lips, her voice dripping into a playful, almost childish tone.

"Yes. Nothing special or anything," I said, shaking my head and shrugging.

"Mmm, to me, it sounds more like a 'date' than a—"

I quickly covered her mouth. "Really! It's not a date, just a friend I'm going out with."

"Whatever. Do Mom and Dad know?" Myra sighed dramatically.

"No, and they don't need to know. You know how they overreact to such things—like when I'm going out at night. Especially Mom."

"True. Don't worry, I won't even tell them."

I pushed her back toward the door. "Great. Now get out. I'll be downstairs in a minute."

Myra went out, and before I could close the door, she peeped in and said, "It's a boy, isn't it?"

I slammed the door shut on her and didn't answer. It *was* a boy—but not really a date. Chris even said so himself.

Time passed quickly, and it was almost 6 p.m. I went back upstairs to get ready and put on my outfit. An hour later, I finished getting myself done and sneaked out of the house to the park. Even though I knew my sister wouldn't tell on me, I still had a little feeling I might get busted. I totally trust Myra, but I don't trust my parents. They always manage to find out what I do—including unnecessary things like "finding out if I've taken a shower" or something. They can be very smart when it comes to figuring out what I'm up to.

Anyway, when I reached the park, it was already 6:10, and Chris was there. He told me to meet him at a small restaurant called *The Comestio*. I entered the restaurant and saw him sitting in the front.

"Hey," I said, sitting down and fixing my outfit one last time.

Chris smiled softly. "Hi. I'm glad you made it."

"Thanks for inviting me. I'm always down to hang with you—you're honestly chill to be around."

"Thanks. You're a chill person too. Even as a friend, you really get me sometimes."

I laid my arms on the table, crossing them. "I think you get me more in life—especially at school yesterday. I really appreciate you helping me out with that plan."

"No problem. Found anyone yet?"

I wanted to say *I found you*—I wished to say that. But I couldn't.

"No, still searching. But for now, I want us to focus on something else."

Chris took the food menu and looked through it. "Sure. Let's start with food. What would you like?"

I also took the other menu and immediately spotted my favourite dish. It was actually the first food Jayson introduced to me at a party restaurant where we celebrated my birthday—vegetable dumpling soup. The taste was excellent. I ordered that with a lemonade drink, and Chris got a lemon chicken dish with a fruit punch.

We ate our dinner and finished our hangout night with a walk back home. It was only seven minutes, so we didn't take long on the way.

But while we were walking, I could feel Chris's arm brushing against mine, and I was shivering inside. It made me want to giggle, and then I did something really stupid—I suddenly took his palm and held it. So tightly he couldn't let go. He didn't let go anyway.

"Your hand is really warm," he chuckled softly.

I smiled and turned away. "Thanks. You didn't pull back."

CHAPTER 10

The night ended when he had to go to his side of the neighborhood. So now, it was just me walking to my street. But when I arrived, I could see someone walking their dog by Jayson's house. It looked like a stranger, but also like Jayson.

I still went nearer to the person to see who it was — and it was definitely him.

Even though I knew he was still angry at me for some reason this week, I decided to at least say hi to him. After all, I couldn't just enter my house while he was right there walking his dog, Perrie.

"Hey, Jayson," I waved slowly at him.

Jayson turned his face from Perrie to me, looking a bit tired.

"Hi."

It was a five-second silence after that — and I didn't like it.

"So, why're you walking Perrie at this time of night?"

"I couldn't take her out for walks this whole week, so I might as well do it now." He shrugged.

I nodded, and then he gripped Perrie's harness, changing his voice to a firm tone. "Where are you coming from at this time?"

"Um…" I sighed, looking all around myself. My outfit looked pretty much obvious for a night hangout. I'm not trying to say Jayson is dumb enough not to realize where I'm coming from, but I was nervous even to tell him about tonight. Besides, he doesn't like Chris — but I do. So will he even accept the truth?

"A hangout with one of my friends at a restaurant in that new park."

Jayson tilted his head, crossing his arms. "I know almost all your friends, Kandis, and most of them are just Nellie and me. So who else are you talking about?"

"Chris." I blurted it out quickly. "Chris and I hung out at a restaurant."

Jayson scoffed and rolled his eyes — and I honestly didn't know why he did that.

"I knew it. Eventually, you and that guy would... go on a date."

I shook my head firmly. "It wasn't a date. Well, I think it kind of was, but like I said, I'm trying to get a boyfriend this year, so maybe Chris—"

"Stop! Just stop," he yelled out. "I don't care about that stupid plan of yours. It's like you lied to me! You said you wouldn't bother talking to boys this school semester — especially ever since that one guy last year broke your heart. You said you also wouldn't bother dating anyone because your parents wouldn't accept it anyway. And it was my idea to get a partner when we started high school!"

Jayson's words caught me off guard. I hadn't expected that — and the shock lingered longer than I cared to admit. But first of all, how could he think I lied? People change their minds. And as a best friend since childhood, he knows I can easily fall in love with guys.

And second of all — why does he even care? Is this the reason he's been so upset with me all week?

"I… I should've known then? I mean, does it matter anymore? I know you don't like Chris, but I still don't get it. Have you been angry at me because of my boyfriend plan, Chris, or something else?"

Jayson let go of Perrie's harness slowly and looked down. "You broke my heart, Kandis. And now you're spending time with some new guy you barely even know. I can tell you like him — probably more than you're willing to admit. You're already thinking about dating, even when this semester was supposed to be about staying focused. You told me, before school even started, that you'd push all the distractions aside and take things seriously this time."

Suddenly, the clouds in the sky turned dark — not just magically, but from behind us. I didn't see or expect it, and soon the droplets of rain came down slowly, then faster. It made the situation feel even more tense.

But I still didn't understand him. Was Chris now unnecessary in my life?

"Wait… how did I break your heart, Jayson?"

I could hear him swallow hard. "I liked you. But you decided to like and love someone else—you don't know as much as you know me. That's how."

"Well, yeah, everyone likes me. I'm a—"

He cut me off, looking up to meet my eyes. "No. I mean… I *liked* you."

All this time, he felt more for me than I realized. My best friend…
was in love with me?

"Wha—what? Since when?"

"Since school started. I thought the feelings would go away, but
they've been getting worse. And now, I don't even need to confess to
you anymore — you clearly want Chris as your soulmate."

Perrie's fur was getting wet, and she shook herself aggressively.
Then Jayson held the harness less tightly.

I was stunned and speechless. How and why did Jayson like me? I
was even surprised he cared so much about me hanging out with Chris.

"Jayson…" I muttered under my breath. I didn't know what to say.
"I don't know how to react to this."

He breathed out loudly. "You don't need to. Because I'm done
with this… and you."

"What are you, breaking this friendship or something?" I joked.

But I was right.

"Yes. I'm sorry, Kandis. It's for the best. As your best friend, I
don't want to hurt your feelings by forcing you to stop talking to Chris
because of me. All I did was tell the truth — but don't take it too
seriously, because I don't think I'll stay the same way."

That's when I broke down. My heart felt like it dropped into my
stomach. My childhood and teenage best friend just ended our
friendship because of… love.

Why? I don't know. Maybe because he's more hurt than he admits
and doesn't want to make it worse — so he crushes it.

But I wasn't letting go. I wasn't letting go of my only guy friend. He was all I had.

"But Jayson… you can't do that. You just can't! I love you."

Jayson shook his head and turned away toward his house. "I do too. But for now… it's best for us to separate. I'm sorry."

He didn't even say goodbye — Perrie did. But it wasn't loud or perfect enough for me to hear and wave back.

He went back to his house, and I did the same. I entered my house with tears dripping slowly down my face. My eyeshadow faded with each drop. The rain made me completely wet and ruined my outfit and makeup.

CHAPTER 11

I flopped on my bed, flat on my stomach, right after I changed into good clothes, burying my whole face—full of tears—on the bed. I just couldn't believe it.

Actually, I could. But I didn't expect it—from my own childhood best friend—to dump our relationship. Over a boy.

Minutes later, after I sobbed for a while, a knock was heard on my door. My parents were both asleep, so it must be Myra.

"Hey, are you awake?" she peeped in.

I nodded, and she came in to sit on the side of my bed.

"I saw you come late. Did the hangout go well?"

"It was… good. I had a fun time with my friend, but—"

She gazed at me. "But? It turned bad later, right?"

"No. When I was coming back home, I met Jayson at his house, walking Perrie—his dog. And since this week started, he's been angry at me for a reason I thought was stupid. But now I regret making the decision." I shook my head and turned away.

"Wait, what decision? And why was he angry? Jayson barely gets angry."

Myra was totally right. I don't remember the last time Jayson got angry—other than this week. Especially at me. And even if he was, it was probably because we were fighting over a stupid thing.

"He was angry because I made this 'get a boyfriend this year' plan for school, and I guess he overreacted and thought it was stupid to do that. But because I didn't listen to him, I asked Chris—my friend that I hung out with tonight—for help, and Jayson… got annoyed."

Myra raised her eyebrows in a daze. "Wow. That's crazy. So now he's, what—stopped talking to you?"

"He decided we should separate and break our friendship. He thinks he knows what's best for me—and he thinks Chris is—but I don't know. I like and want both of them!" I put my hands over my head dramatically.

"Well… if you're ever confused about love, you should get therapy, honey." She yawned theatrically.

I hit her shoulder lightly with the back of my fist. "Stop! I'm being serious. It's not just love—it's a friendship I never want to separate from."

"Listen, I've been in this situation before. I've lost a lot of friends—it's no big deal for me. But you—I get it. And you can fix it. I know."

"I know too. But I don't know if it will work; my plans never do. Just like the boyfriend one." I sighed tiredly.

"Oh. I thought that Chris guy you went out with tonight was going to be the one."

I chuckled softly. "Please, Chris is just… there for an 'in-case situation.' I'm still going to keep talking to him, but for now, I need to set my mind on my lost best friend."

I honestly felt an ache in me when I said that last sentence. I know he made his decision to separate us—but I haven't. I'm still thinking about it, because, definitely, I haven't and won't lose my best friend.

"Good. Don't worry, though; everything will turn out fine in the end. Jayson will come back to you. That, for sure, I know."

"Thanks. And for now, I think we should head to bed."

Myra came closer to me and kissed my forehead softly. I felt such comfort from that—from a really good sister.

"Thanks, Myra."

Myra smiled genuinely and went out of the room. I closed my eyes and went straight to sleep.

CHAPTER 12

The next day was a Sunday. I woke with a heaviness still clinging to me—tired and drained. After whispering my morning prayers and flipping through my daily scriptures, I remembered we wouldn't be going to church today; the car was still in the mechanic's shop. I slipped into my yellow summer jumpsuit—the one with soft white stripes—and headed downstairs, only to find Uncle Eddie still in the house, surprisingly.

I didn't expect it. Even though he said he could only stay for three days and had hung out with me and Myra, we'd only gone out on Friday, after school, to the city. And I'd overheard my dad talking about work stuff with him before, so I thought he'd be with Dad, working on business and all.

"Hey, Kandis. You're awake early." Uncle Eddie turned to me from the lounge room, smiling as his dimples popped out.

I put my hands behind me, ambling to his side and onto the couch. "Yeah, I mean, I'm still a bit tired, but I decided to wake up anyway."

"That's good. You can be an early bird like your mom." He chuckled under his breath.

My mom was an early bird, but she never liked people in the house waking up before her. She always wanted everything in the house organized before anyone else did it. It's like her job was to do everything by herself—without anyone's help or interference.

And I barely woke up early in the morning because, normally, Myra came to wake me up anytime I overslept. That happens because I sometimes stay up late. So I wouldn't really call myself an early bird.

"I wouldn't take that as a compliment, Uncle Eddie. But why're you here alone? Where's everyone?"

He leaned back on the couch. "Your parents and sister have gone to a conference meeting at Myra's activity club, using a cab. And I was asked to take care of you while they're there."

I crossed my feet together, sitting stiffly on the couch. Uncle Eddie noticed my expression, and his eyes roamed over me.

"Are you okay, Kandis?"

"Yeah, I'm fine," I said, still not moving.

"You look frozen. You normally roam around the house and jump up and down anytime I'm here. Why does it feel quiet now? You're not quiet around me."

I sighed, not sure if I should tell Uncle Eddie the truth. Would he even care? He barely knew Jayson—and had only met him once or twice. So did Jayson. I didn't know if it was a really good idea to tell him my problems.

"I… I don't know. There's a reason I'm playing the part of the quiet, strange girl right now. But I'm not sure if I can tell you—or anyone—the problem I'm having."

"Hey," he said, his voice softer now, "I'm your uncle for a reason. I'm not just here to crack jokes and play the over-the-top funny guy. You can tell me your secrets—anything you need to say."

I really appreciated what Uncle Eddie was doing for me right now. He's the only fun, positive, and good family member here. Though Myra is too, he's way better.

"Alright." I trusted him. "My best friend has been angry at me since this week started. One reason is that I made a 'get a boyfriend' plan, and he didn't approve at all. Either he was jealous, or he thought it was a bad idea for me because it might lead to trouble."

"A 'get a boyfriend' plan? Kandis, that's a bit heavy and far for a girl your age!" He chuckled.

I folded my lips tight, not saying anything. That wasn't a joke— my separated friendship with Jayson isn't a joke.

"Sorry, I didn't mean it as an offense. But if I'm being serious, getting a boyfriend this early isn't a good idea. And honestly, things like that can quietly pull your focus away from what really matters right now. You're only fifteen—still growing, still learning who you are.

"This isn't the time to rush into something just because it feels exciting or expected. You've got dreams to chase, goals to reach, and so many chances to build the life you want. There will be time for love later—when you're ready and when it makes sense. But for now? Let that plan go. It's not what you need."

CHAPTER 13

S o Jayson was right. Okay, but so what? I'm done with that plan already—not just because Jayson told me to, but because my plan kind of worked. Chris is now in my life. Even though Jayson has now made me think about his feelings for me. I mean, two guys over one girl?

"But you're still innocent. Jayson doesn't have much right to just get angry at you because of a love plan you made. That always happens when teenagehood comes. I get you—it's okay to have feelings for someone. And if Jayson isn't okay with it, then… maybe he's jealous."

"Well, that's weird. I think the right word is just annoyance. Because ever since I started talking and hanging out with my friend—whom I have a crush on—he's been really upset and ignorant. That's one of the reasons he's so angry at me." I crossed my arms.

"But don't you see it? Maybe it's not just annoyance or anger. He's definitely jealous, though. I know it because I've been in that situation before. A lot of guys get that way."

That shocked me. Jayson has never been jealous of me. He's my best friend—so that can't happen. But it's kind of possible, because he technically confessed his feelings for me. So… he's been jealous that I hung out with a different guy than him because he likes me.

"I guess that makes sense. I mean, I get every single piece of this. But he didn't just get angry at me because of my crush and the boyfriend plan. Last night, he also confessed his feelings for me, and just ended our friendship because he was…"

"He was hurt," Uncle Eddie finished. "He didn't want to make it look like you have to pick between him and your crush, so he broke the friendship."

But I have to pick between them. I love them both.

"Is there anything I can do, then? I already miss him, and I want my best friend back." My voice cracked.

Uncle Eddie smiled softly. "I have three things to say to you—you can pick one or leave all."

What did he mean by that? Picking one of his absurd ideas is like picking between my best friend and my crush.

"Either date your best friend, and befriend your crush."
"Either date your crush, and befriend your best friend."
"Or, better yet, don't date any of them—just be friends."

Look, I don't mean to sound rude, but most of those suggestions felt off—strange, even. I knew from the start they wouldn't work. I can't just force myself to date my best friend and pretend to befriend my crush just because I casually have feelings for Jayson or want him back. And flipping it the other way around—dating my crush while trying to stay close to Jayson—would only make things messier between us. It's not that simple.

The thing is, I want Chris and Jayson, but I don't want to date either of them. Even though I like Chris, Jayson is now making me rethink my feelings.

"I don't know, Uncle Eddie... there's a fifty percent chance it won't work. But the thing is, I want both of them, not just one."

"You want to... date both of them?" Uncle Eddie said it like a statement.

It seemed he didn't understand what I meant about the broken relationship I'm going through.

"No, I want them back in my life. Maybe not as love partners, but just... friends."

I kind of hate saying that. Because I wanted to date someone, at least before this school semester ends. I really think I have that experience of being someone's own. But I don't even have my one and only friend anymore, nor a partner. So I have nothing.

"Well, Kandis, if you really want those two back—go get them." He said it like it meant something.

It gave me a little hope, though. But I needed more than just hope.

"How? Jayson has probably planned on ignoring me now, till school ends."

"What about that crush of yours?"

I sighed—not tired, not relieved, but unbothered. "Uncle Eddie, Chris is perfectly fine with me. We're friends, and we literally talk all the time. I like him, but Jayson's kind of making me change my mind."

"Kandis, don't let that get to you. If you really like that guy, it's fine. Jayson departed from you because he wanted you to know he doesn't want you to put a friendship relationship between a love relationship you're just starting and want to continue. But remember—don't go too far with that."

But I just said I'm thinking of changing my mind. I might not have full love feelings for Chris anymore. But I also don't want that. And Jayson—or any other best friend—wouldn't just quit a long friendship over love. He's smart enough to know that.

"It's probably just his love for me, Uncle. I need to fix it, though—that's all."

Uncle Eddie shifted away from me a bit. "And will you actually do it?"

Well, I wasn't thinking of giving up right away.

"Yes. It's a promise—to fix my relationship with Jayson and my feelings for Chris."

CHAPTER 14

Right after that talk, I went back to my room and sat at my reading desk. It was the only thing that could settle my thoughts. I didn't want to spiral into everything I was feeling—not again. I'm still just a child, and if I'm going to fix this, I'll need time.

So I took one of my favourite books that I haven't finished reading yet, *Courtesy of Cupid*, and turned to the middle page, continuing where I left off.

After a while, I realized I *do* need to fix this. Not later in the day, not next year, but right now—anytime I have. I need to do something. Maybe not a plan; I know the made-up plans I have are what cause breakups. So instead, the next day at school, I decided to try and talk to both of the boys who were making my life so hard.

But Jayson wasn't bothering to help. What I mean is, anytime we finished a class, we'd always see or meet each other in the hallway, and he wouldn't even try to look at me. It's like he wanted to, but didn't want to cause a scene. Even though I did.

But of course, I didn't give up.

After the last class—Art—I walked to the foyer, trying to find my friends so we could possibly walk back home. And then I spotted Jayson at his locker, packing up his things. I knew this was my chance to go talk to him, even if it was the last minute.

But then, unexpectedly, Chris noticed me walking around and stopped me. He pulled me lightly to one of the lockers and held my palm.

"Hey, Kandis."

I hesitated to talk. I just kept looking at Jayson, who was in front of us. Luckily, he didn't see us. But I really didn't have time to do this with Chris.

"Uh… hey, Chris." I faked a smile.

It seemed he knew I wasn't comfortable because he tilted his head and frowned, rubbing his palms against mine. "Is everything okay with you?"

"Yeah—actually, no, not really."

I suddenly remembered Jayson wasn't the only one I needed to apologize to or fix things with. Chris also needed an explanation. I mean, I'd feel really awful once he found out Jayson likes me.

"What is it?" He breathed near my ear, and it made me stop thinking. "You can always tell me anything."

I somehow wanted and didn't want to tell him what was going on—if that even made sense. But I just couldn't. I already broke my first-ever guy friend's heart. I didn't want to break another! Even if he actually needed to know the truth, I didn't feel like he would want to know. After all, he's my *maybe crush*. But I also couldn't lie.

"Uh… I need to talk to you about something going on with me and Jayson." I slowly took my palm away from his.

"Jayson? Your best friend? What's up with you and him?"

Chris asked it like I wasn't supposed to be up to something with him. I mean, I wasn't—but Jayson made it *look* like I was.

"We stopped being friends. Jayson decided we should separate, which I think is just a *break*, and now we aren't talking. Well, he won't talk to me." I fidgeted with my hands.

"Oh, that's so sudden. Nellie told me about you guys not acting like 'best friends' around each other anyway, so…" Chris shrugged.

Wait—Nellie knows?

Does this mean Jayson told almost everyone I don't want to know about this? Like his family?

"Really? Jayson is already spreading the news?"

Right when I said that, I heard a small slam on a locker in front of me—and it was Jayson, who had just finished packing his stuff for home.

I turned to him, then to Chris, then back at Jayson, who passed by us, holding his backpack tightly.

"Hey, Jayson!" Chris waved, turning his head to him.

I froze—completely. I could feel Jayson's frustration and anger in the air. It was like I could even hear him breathe hard. I'd messed up so bad; I was scared to talk to him.

He didn't answer back, of course. He wasn't even paying attention when Chris said hi. But then he turned to us mid-conversation and folded his lips shut, making his face look like a hard rock—cold and unwilling to be there. Then he walked out of the school.

That quickly made me turn back to Chris and tell him everything—how Jayson had a crush on me, how he was super angry, and how all of it made me feel humiliated and uneasy. I didn't even want to think about having a love partner anymore.

"What—you mean you don't want to date me anymore?" he asked, frowning with a pitiful look that made me feel bad.

But this wasn't funny; what he said felt like a joke. We never even went on an *actual* date, did we?

"No? We never dated, though—we just hung out on a Saturday night." I held onto my backpack strap.

"Well, I thought of it as a date. Like, you know, the start of our relationship?" He looked down. "But I guess not. You don't realize it because you don't think of it as that."

I took his hand, rubbing it against mine. "No! I mean, I *do* have a crush on you. But with Jayson making our friendship seem worse, and it's on my mind all the time, it makes me forget about… our starting relationship."

"Just say it." He shook his head.

I squeezed his hand—unintentionally. "What?"

"Just say you don't like me. Since Jayson confessed that he has feelings for you, you've been obsessed—thinking that because he's your best friend, and that he just separated from you, now you want him back, and—"

"Chris! That's my problem, not yours."

I tried to sound calm, but I wasn't. I didn't want to lie, but I didn't want to tell the truth either. Maybe—or maybe not—I have a crush on Jayson, too. But he's my best friend; there's no way.

Still, Chris needs to get this. I might not have a huge crush on him like I did before—when he was a total newbie.

CHAPTER 15

"You need to just… give me some time." I turned my head away, still holding his hand. "I need to fix, resettle, and think about this situation between me and my one and true best friend first. Then we can—"

"Then we can what? Go back to the same restaurant, redo the hangout, and pretend like we're in love—and also act like nothing happened this week?" Chris raised his voice a bit.

I blinked rapidly, not knowing what to say. This was so confusing, messed up, and crazy—especially hard to deal with.

"Like I said, just admit it. If not, then we can just go our own ways, like how you and Jayson did. I'm sorry, Kandis."

He removed his hands from mine and left my side—and the school. Leaving me alone there, the last person just standing in the foyer, overthinking my thoughts. Mostly about me being devastated.

Back at home, I wasn't distracted by anyone in the house. My parents and Myra realized I wasn't feeling good today. I don't know if they know about my breakup with two of my guy friends, or maybe Myra told them about Saturday night, but I barely cared. I was worrying about my life problems—not just today's, but all of them right now.

Including Uncle Eddie being gone. He went back to his home this morning. I didn't get to see or say goodbye to him for the last time, but I still thought of that as something to worry about. Because without him, who was going to help me with this terrible issue I'm going through?

Then, this thought immediately came to my mind while I was in my room—when Uncle tried to advise me on my issue. Though the part where he said I could befriend one and date the other was weird, I didn't think much about it. I don't want to make one jealous, mad, or upset.

Because now I understand what Jayson meant. It's not like he wants to date me or anything; he just likes me. Maybe as a crush or a best friend. But what he wants is for me never to treat Chris like a full-on, forever friend or partner—and leave him like that. He just doesn't want me to put another person in our long friendship. Especially a guy. And he never liked Chris, so… he's too upset about it.

But as for Chris, I know he really likes me and wants to date me. But I don't want that. I like him, but not enough to say, *I want to be with him.* Chris is a really good guy though—I can tell we can be good, in fact, such close friends. But I can't even do that because both of them are angry at me.

Just because of love.

So, I decided to just do the last advice tip Uncle Eddie gave me: *don't date any of them, and just be friends.* Honestly, it wasn't a bad tip. For someone like Uncle Eddie, who is so dramatic and crazy for no reason, it's really impressive for him to give me such advice. I never would've thought of that.

But what if it doesn't work? I'm not sure if Jayson and Chris would even agree to it. I was nervous about this. That's why I didn't even bother thinking of such advice to fix this situation.

But now that I've found the solution, I need to do it. Like, I have to do it now—which meant getting my school clothes off, wearing a casual home fit, going out of the house, and starting to walk to a nearby park.

It was like a plan—not made up—because I had it solved quickly.

CHAPTER 16

So, here was what I was going to do. I took out my phone and texted Chris and Jayson to meet me at Prakie Park—the same place where I'd had that hangout with Chris at the restaurant. It showed that Chris saw the message, but Jayson didn't. I know he probably saw the notification and all, but I don't think he cared to come to the park. And I really wanted them to come; if not, this advice and plan weren't going to work.

I reached the park before either of the guys did. But ten minutes later, Chris came and saw me sitting on the bench. His face was blank with boredom, like he didn't even want to be here.

I waved and got up to say hi. "You came. Thanks."

"I just want to know the reason." He shrugged.

I folded my lips and nodded. I didn't want him to know the plan yet. It was like a surprise—but since he and Jayson had to think about it and agree, they both needed to be here to listen, understand, and for once, know what I meant by *the boyfriend plan.*

"Uh… let's wait for Jayson first."

After a while, Jayson came. He was a bit late, but at least he cared enough to show up.

I told them to sit on the bench and just hear me out. I explained the whole boyfriend plan—that I wasn't chasing love; I just wanted someone to talk to, hang out with, and spend time around.

Jayson didn't seem to agree. He thought the idea was pointless—and maybe even feared that Chris might take me away from him.

And Chris… I know I've said it before, but I could tell he was upset. Maybe it was the way I kept revolving around Jayson at school, when all he wanted was to talk about *us*.

"I just want to be friends with you both, for now," I said, changing the topic. "And until I get what I want, can the status quo remain?"

Chris turned to Jayson, and Jayson looked at him too. Then they both faced me.

"Kandis, whether we're friends or not, I just don't want you out of my life." Chris showed me his soft, meaningful smile.

I was pleased by that—finally, someone could agree with this plan. "Thanks, Chris. We can be just… good friends."

But now it was Jayson's turn. What was he going to say? Would he agree? Deny it? Or stay angry at me?

I was really worried and scared. I didn't want my best friend away from my life. But now that I'd decided to befriend both of them officially, he couldn't say no.

"Well? What's your decision, Jayson?" I asked, lowering my voice.

He still didn't say anything, and I didn't know what to do.

"Please, you can't just turn me away like that. I love you—since I was a kid—and I know you do too. We've been friends since I learned how to say words. And I'm sorry I tried to take you away by adding

Chris into my life, but I want both of you to be friends with me, Jayson."

I said that from my heart, soul, and body. This time, even if he said no, I was just going to slap him and take Chris away as my new love partner.

"Okay, okay. I agree to this friend status being quo." He nodded, chuckling under his breath. "I've already forgiven you, Kandis. You were the only one who stood by me when I was a kid—how could I ever push you away? I just needed to know if you'd ever try to come back. I mean, I wanted you back."

Chris jumped in before I could respond. "Wait—you still like Kandis?"

I focused my eyes and thoughts only on Jayson this time. Was he going to say what I thought he was going to say?

"Um... no, not really. I decided to let the feelings go away. She's my best friend—I can't date her." He said it like a joke.

Now *that's* what I wanted to hear—the real Jayson, confessing that he didn't like me.

"Exactly! Because you guys are just friends!" I hugged them both softly, then pulled back quickly.

For now, it seemed everything *was* and *is* going well. I just hope that as I grow up, this problem won't happen again. Because I already have my real friends: Chris, Jayson, and, of course, Nellie.

BETWEEN THE LANES

"Some bonds form quietly–hidden in routine,

revealed in time."

CHAPTER 1

D ear diary, I was *this* close to winning—until a red car sped past me and claimed the finish line like it had wings.

"Ugh, seriously?" I muttered, annoyed. "I could've had that... if that flashy red show-off didn't swerve in like he owned the track."

Still confused by how it happened so fast, I checked the leaderboard. His name was Prince_Icondash101. Yeah, don't even ask. That's probably the weirdest name I've ever seen for a guy.

I didn't dwell on it too long, though. I shut the game off and headed downstairs for dinner.

It's just me, Dad, and Mermie—my little rescue pup. We're not exactly a big family, since Dad never talks about Mom. Every time I bring her up, he either changes the story or gives me that same line: *"You'll understand when you're older."*

But I'm fifteen now. When exactly does *'older'* start?

Anyway, I decided to leave that aside and just eat my dinner. While I was at the table, eating my elegant spaghetti carbonara, Dad was at the stove dishing out his food.

He turned to me, holding his plate, and said, "So, the school called me this morning."

I dropped my fork.

Uh-oh. Did he find out about me cheating on the science test?

He sat down beside me, but he didn't look angry or disgruntled.

"And they said a new student was coming to the school," he said calmly.

I interrupted him, still worried he'd found out about the test. "Wait—this isn't about the… test?"

"No?" he replied, confused. "What test?"

Oh, great. He doesn't know. For a second, my chest tightened so hard I thought I'd crack—I was *sure* he found out I cheated on that science test. The guilt had been sitting in my stomach all week, curling up like bad food.

But the way he spoke this morning—calm and casual—made me realize he had no clue. Still… I couldn't help but wonder if this conversation was about to take a sharp turn.

"Nothing… keep going." I faked a smile.

"Anyway, as I was saying, a new student is coming to your class," Dad continued. "And they need three kids from your class to assist him around the school."

"Every day?" I glanced at him.

"No, just for now—until they get used to the school."

"Okay, so why tell me?" I took another bite of my food.

"They need *you* to come, Elle. And two other kids. You probably know them."

"But I don't want to! It's literally summer break. Can't the other kids just do it without me?"

"No. I agreed with the school, so they're expecting you. I can't say no now."

Well, Dad—maybe you should've thought about telling me first before agreeing to something I *definitely* didn't want to do. But I didn't argue; I just finished my food and went back to my room.

CHAPTER 2

The next morning, I pushed myself to wake up early—something I hadn't done in a while. Ever since that little girl on the bus whispered something to her mom, I hadn't been able to shake it off. I didn't catch the full sentence, but I swear I heard the word *"fat."* That alone was enough to put me in this quiet haze.

So, I got up, took a warm shower, and pulled on my oversized white sweater and favorite black shorts—something that felt like comfort and effort at once. "A little makeup wouldn't hurt," I mumbled, dusting my cheeks with my Sephora blush, the one that always made me feel a bit more like myself. Just as I reached for my lip balm, a sudden shout came from downstairs.

"Elle, we need to go!"

Then I realized we were going to the school for the new–student–assistant thing. I guess no exercise then.

I jogged downstairs to see Dad already heading out of the house. When we were on the way to school, nothing about the building caught me off guard—it was exactly how I remembered it. No new paint, no updated garden, not even a cleaner sign. I had secretly hoped they'd fix up a few things—maybe change the walls or give the place a fresh look—but no. The same building. Same hallway smell. Same dull *"Parkland High"* sign hanging crooked above the door like it always did.

As soon as we stepped inside and headed to the principal's office, I noticed two familiar faces already waiting—Samantha and Joan from my class.

"Sorry," Dad started. "Are we late?"

"Oh no, not at all! Please have a seat." Principal Wilkinson smiled.

We sat next to the two other students, and while we were waiting for the new student, I took out my iPad and started playing a racing game. It's actually called *MS Car Racing,* and it was originally made in the city where I was born and used to live—Marseille, where my mom probably is…

Anyway, after waiting for about fifteen minutes for the new student, they finally arrived. And it was a boy.

A tall, lean boy with that effortlessly French look stood just a few feet away, wearing a watercolor–patterned shirt that somehow made basketball shorts look classy. His cologne—soft, clean, a little addictive—lingered in the air between us. I could've stared for hours. There was something about him that made it hard to look away. Beside him stood a woman who had to be his mom, her expression tense, like she was holding onto a worry she didn't want to share out loud.

"Sorry, we're late. There was a huge traffic jam on the way."

"Oh, no worries!" Principal Gabrielle stood up. We all greeted him and his mother. Then the principal took five minutes to talk about his class, extracurricular activities, and responsibilities he needed to know.

Afterward, the principal didn't linger to chat and decided to start the assistant thing. But it was just us—the three of us. The parents didn't come. So, we went out and started taking him to the main classes, like the science lab.

"So, I'm Samantha. Sam is easier for me, though," Samantha said, entering the lab.

No one else said anything, so I added, "And I'm Elle… and that's Joan." I pointed to the boy beside the student, knowing he wouldn't say his name because he was busy texting on his phone.

"Oh," the new student muttered. "Cool. I'm Travis."

Well, that's a cool name for a boy like that.

CHAPTER 3

After checking out the lab, we decided to go to the gym. But before we could get there, Joan put his phone back in his pocket and tapped Samantha on the shoulder.

"Race you to the gym!"

Samantha startled a little but still yelled, "Joan! You cheater!"

They both took off running before us, leaving me and Travis walking alone. I felt like melting. It was so quiet, and we weren't saying anything.

"So..." Travis looked down. "How long have you been in this school?"

I hadn't been here long—just under three years, really.

"Uh... just two years. I'm a sophomore," I said, placing my hands behind me.

"Oh, okay. This is my fifth school, actually."

"Wait, really? How?" I turned fully to face him.

"My parents got divorced when I was in first grade. That was my second school. And since then... it's just been one move after another. Every time I try to settle in, we're packing up again. So I might move from this school... again." He frowned, eyes drifting away from mine.

"Oh, I'm sorry—about the divorce, I mean. But don't worry, this school's actually fun. You might end up loving it so much you won't even want to leave."

"Yeah, well, that's not really my call. It's my mom's. I live with her now."

"Do you… ever visit your dad?"

"Sometimes. Usually just on weekends," he shrugged.

Poor guy. He's kind of like me—growing up with only one parent. The only difference is… at least he still sees both of them. I've never even seen my mom. And maybe I never will.

After that talk, we all entered the gym and showed Travis around. We wanted to play a little game of basketball, but we didn't have enough time, so we just left and went to the last class—our homeroom.

By tomorrow, this is where we'll be staying. Practically learning.

"Wow, this room is big. Twice the size of my former class in my old school," Travis uttered.

"Yeah, I know," Samantha said. "It's not much of a surprise, though. Almost all the classes in this school are big—*very* big!"

"Wow, I can't wait to see some tomorrow." Travis smiled.

We all decided to race back to the office, just for fun. Surprisingly, Samantha and Joan were trailing behind while Travis and I were side by side, competing to see who'd take the lead. I slid past him at one point, accidentally making him stumble a bit—but before I could even check if he was okay, he'd already gotten back on his feet and dashed ahead. He beat me to the office door in seconds. I stood there, breathless, my chest rising fast—but what confused me the most was how he recovered so quickly and still managed to win.

"How—did… how the heck did you do that? I literally almost passed you!"

"I've been running track and field my whole life, so it isn't new or hard for me," he panted a little.

He opened the door for us, but before we could enter, he asked, "But how did you run so fast? You were like a cheetah! I was scared I couldn't pass you for a second."

"Uh…" I stammered, thinking he would laugh if I told him about my point of view. "I don't know, I just love running. Sometimes I want to be a racer—like a car racer, or a runner."

His eyebrows lifted, full of surprise, like he wanted to say something—but he couldn't, because Principal had already told us to come in.

We all said goodbye and left the office.

Although I expected the principal to bring up the test news to my dad, she didn't. And it's not like I'm desperate to hide it or scared of him finding out—but almost everyone else already knows. My teacher, my best friend, even some kids in other classes. The only person left in the dark is him. And he's never liked being the last to know, especially when it's something I kept to myself.

I guess… for now, I got lucky.

CHAPTER 4

Anyway, on our way back to the car, I heard Travis call out my name. I turned back, and he came up to me.

"Sorry, I just wanted to thank you for the assistance. Now I know where I'll go tomorrow."

I smiled and said, "No worries. See you tomorrow."

"Yeah, bye!"

Honestly, I could feel my face heating up. I mean, this was probably the first time a guy like Travis—not just cute but actually cool—ever spoke to me. Like, really spoke. A full-on conversation. And I wasn't sure what felt crazier—the way he talked to me like we'd known each other for years, or the way I kind of liked it.

That same night, I wanted to play a bit of the *MS Car Racing* game before going to bed. So, I set up a ten-minute timer, because if I didn't, I'd probably wake up late tomorrow—and my dad would rage about it.

I immediately changed into my PJs and went straight to the computer. As I was racing in *MS Car Racing* and seriously focused on the track, a red car sped past me and almost won the game. And it looked like the same car from the last time I played. When it ended, I asked him to 1v1 me, and he agreed.

While we were getting our cars ready, I took a sip of my water. Then he turned on his voice chat and said,

"So… are you shocked that I beat you… again?"

I nearly choked on my water. Two reasons why: one, his voice changer—way deeper than I imagined—and two, no, I wasn't shocked he won again. He only kept winning because I wasn't taking it seriously.

I switched on my mic and softened my voice—not deep like his, more calm and casual—and said, "No? I'm just… stunned. I mean, a guy like you, with a name like *'Prince_IconDash101,'* winning that fast? Impressive."

"Eh," he muttered, pretending to be grumpy. "Just a trick I got from my dad. He used to be a pro at running—and pretty decent at car racing in video games."

"So you're following in his footsteps?"

"Not exactly. I want to be like him. One day."

"Well, with skills like that, I wouldn't doubt it."

He chuckled but didn't say anything else, so I assumed he'd turned his mic off. I did the same and focused back on the game.

The race began.

I was already clocking 180 mph, but he was cruising at 200. At that point, yeah—I was officially provoked. No way was I losing this time.

CHAPTER 5

I activated my Hot Wheels, used a couple of tricks to slow him down, and flew past him. Not long after, his voice chat clicked back on—he must've been just as shocked.

"Whoa! How'd you pass me like that?"

I didn't answer because I was focused—and I can't be interrupted anytime I'm focused. Especially by a boy (with the weirdest name ever) who beat me twice. Before he could try to pass me and win again, I briskly finished the race and crossed the line in first place.

I turned my voice chat back on and said, "I guess it's a skill."

He laughed, and we ended the game. But it didn't end there. He politely asked for my number—and of course, I said yes. Honestly, I'd wanted his number from the start. There was just something cool about him.

After that, I shut off my computer and flopped onto my bed tiredly. But just as I glanced at the time—curious how many minutes I had left before bed—my phone lit up. It was him. The race guy. Already calling. And thank God… it was a voice call.

"Hey," he said first.

"Hi," I replied in my best girly voice ever.

"Are you free to chat?" he asked.

I checked my timer and realized I only had five minutes left. But a quick call wouldn't hurt.

"Yeah," I muttered. "So, are you surprised I beat you this time?"

He chuckled. "I guess—but I knew you'd eventually win. I don't expect girls like you to be *that* horrible at games like this."

I laughed so hard I thought I'd die from it.

"You're kind of a funny guy."

"Really?"

"Yeah."

"Anyway, I haven't gotten your name." He tried to change the subject, but I wasn't ready for it.

"Oh… um." I didn't want to give him my real name—especially since I didn't know him that well.

"It's fine if you don't want to tell me," he said quickly. "You can fake it and make one up."

"Uh… it's Els." I already knew it was a horrible name.

"Cool. I'm PrinceTrev."

I laughed again. "PrinceTrev? That's so made up—and fake."

"I know. I thought of it last minute."

"Nice. But I gotta go. Um… text you tomorrow afternoon?"

"Okay. I'm only free at that time anyway."

"Alright, bye."

"See ya."

I'll admit—I had a good time talking with him. Like I said, he's a pretty cool guy.

CHAPTER 6

This day was the day I was going to school… again. I was pretty happy and a little annoyed because, one: school sessions are the worst here and pretty much boring; and two: I get to meet my best friend, who has always made me smile since third grade. She's practically my sister.

That morning, I decided to wear light blue flared jeans and a white shirt with a black cross on it. I wanted to put on makeup, but I knew it would make me kind of ugly since I can't do makeup well. But of course, I had to put on my special makeup—the Sephora blush powder.

Anyway, as I went downstairs for breakfast, I saw Dad in the kitchen with a depressed face. I rushed to his side, worried, and asked, "Dad, what's wrong?"

He looked at me with a crooked smile.
"Oh, nothing, sweetheart. Just eat your food and get to school quickly."

"But, Dad, I can tell something's wrong."

"Just…" he murmured, "eat your food and get to school."

I obeyed and quickly finished my fried egg and mint tea. Afterward, I put on my jacket and boots and waved at Dad. But all he did was give me a half smile. Right then, I knew something was wrong with him—because he definitely wasn't himself.

I was at my locker at school when someone tapped my shoulder. I turned to see my best friend, Marla.

"Hey, Elle," she smiled.

I quickly forgot about Dad's problem, and my spirit lifted.

"Marls! How've you been? And how'd the vacation go?"

"I've never been happier, Elle! I had so much fun—I went to a waterpark, then a camp trip, and traveled to London! I almost forgot today was the first day of school."

I was surprised. No wonder she barely texted or called me over the break.

"Wow…" I mumbled.

"What about you? Did you enjoy your summer?"

"Uh…" I mean, sure—I had a bit of fun. A couple of racing games here and there, saw my grandparents twice. But compared to Marla? Not even close.

"Nothing much," I said casually. "Just visited my grandparents and had a little mukbang with my cousins."

"Whoa, cool!"

I already knew she said *cool* just to make me feel good about my summer, because I never have as much fun as she does during breaks. She knows whatever I do in summer—or even winter—is low-average fun. She just says *cool* all the time because she's that type of best friend.

"Um…" Marla turned to the kids walking by with a confused look. "Who's that?"

"Huh?" I closed my locker.

"A freshman or something?"

She was looking at the new kid, and I could tell she was already into him.

"Oh, that's Travis—the new guy in my class."

"Whoa…" She lowered her mouth, opening it slowly.

"Why'd you ask?" I crossed my arms.

"Nothing! Uh, gotta get to class. See you at lunch!"

She ran upstairs, still glancing at Travis, who was entering the homeroom—making me remember I also had to be there.

CHAPTER 7

"Okay, class, so today we're going to do a Physics project—and it includes only two partners," Mrs. Jean said.

Oh, great. So without my best friend here, who will I partner with?

"And the project is about the studies we learned from gravity and mass last semester," she continued.

Wait, what? How the heck are we going to do a project on gravity and mass that we learned three months ago? And we just started school—why are we doing a project so fast?

Right after Mrs. Jean talked about what we were supposed to do for the project, we thought we should start picking out our partners. But she suggested she should do it—and I knew that meant a terrible partner for me.

"Okay, Elle," she looked at me. I really hoped it wasn't someone who would bother me. "Your partner is Travis."

Oh. I actually wasn't expecting that.

"Both of you should start working on your project at one of your desks."

I was kind of—and not kind of—surprised. I mean, Travis? The new kid was my project partner? Although, I was lucky it wasn't one of those annoying boys in the class. I took out my notebook, pen, and Physics book and waited for Travis to come to my desk, because I was totally not sitting at or around his desk; it already looked… messy and crazy, since he was sitting near the dirtiest, most revolting part of the room.

After some time, he finally came over with his notebook and pen.

"I guess we're doing the project at your desk?" he said, sitting slowly on the chair beside me.

"Yeah," I smiled.

I flipped open the Physics textbook and said, "Since the project's focused on gravity and mass, I'm pretty sure chapter five, page thirty-nine, explains the physics side of it best."

"Right, that's good. But we still need more than just the physics. We need the meaning—like proof, perspective… something that actually helps us grasp it better," he said, eyes scanning the page. I frowned. "Wait, isn't all of that already in this chapter? I thought it all kind of tied into the same idea of physics?"

"Not exactly. Just because two things fall under the same subject doesn't mean they carry the same meaning," he replied calmly.

I tilted my head, confused. "Huh?"

He reached over, grabbed both of our water bottles, and held them up. "Look at these."

I blinked. "Okay…?"

"Your bottle's plastic. It's meant for multiple types of liquids— juice, water, even oil. My bottle's metal—it's built to hold hot drinks or water and insulate it. Yours can be recycled; mine, not really. See the difference? Same function, different design, different understanding."

I stared for a moment, just stunned.

He set the bottles down and asked, "Make sense now?"

Honestly, how does he know this stuff? The way he explained it—so calmly, like he just knew how to connect science to real life. "Um..." I stammered. "Since when were you this good at physics?" He laughed. "I don't know if it's physics or just... observation. Maybe intelligence decided to visit me today."

Wow. Did he just subtly call me dumb?

"Okay, genius, can we please go back to the project now?" I said with a fake laugh.

He nodded. "Sure."

But just as we tried to turn the page to the section on mass, the lunch bell rang.

I sighed and started packing up my books when he tapped my shoulder.

"So... I'll see you tomorrow?" he asked.

I blinked. "Tomorrow? We have gym after lunch, remember?"

His face went blank. "Wait—we do?"

"Yeah, we're on the same schedule the whole semester."

"Ohhh, so... classmates forever?"

I laughed harder than I meant to—loud enough that people probably heard me in the hall.

"I guess so," I said, still giggling. "But come on, Travis, seriously. Let's go eat."

And just like that, he ran out of the classroom like some circus clown and left me wheezing. That boy was something else—ridiculous, but hilarious.

CHAPTER 8

I was trying to find a table in the cafeteria when Marla waved at me to come.

"Where have you been?" she asked, moving aside for me to sit.

"I was busy talking to Travis," I said, sitting down.

"Travis?" she uttered.

"Yeah, you know, the new kid, the one you kept staring at the—"

"Shh!" She put her hand on my mouth. "You don't have to say it, I know."

"Okay…" I couldn't believe my best friend was falling in love with a new guy she'd never even seen or talked to in her whole life.

"So," she turned to me with a smoothie in her hand, "what were you two chatting about in class?"

I shrugged. "Nothing. We were just doing a project, and he kept making random jokes."

"Were they funny?"

"Um… yeah? Okay, why these types of questions?"

"Oh, nothing. Just wanna know more about this Travis guy."

"Oh, really? Well, Marla, if you really like this guy, you should just talk to him, because I know you *do* like him. Maybe at the end of school, you should try saying hi to him."

Marla made a confused face and said, "What are you talking about? You think I like him?"

"Yeah… don't you?" I opened my lunchbox.

"No. Listen, just because you kept seeing me talking about him doesn't mean I like him."

"Oh… really?" I folded my arms, not believing her words.

Marla rubbed her neck and looked down. "Yeah, my mom and my sister thought I had a bad taste in boys, so when they found out a new boy was coming to the school, they thought I should try talking and hanging out with him."

I didn't say anything, and she continued, "But even when I tried to see if it would work, I realized you were talking to him a lot, so I just quit."

"Oh… well, just for your information, I don't really have a taste in Travis, but I'm sure you'll find your guy."

"Thanks." She gave me her usual smile.

Back home, I came in to see Dad in the living room—dressed like he was going to a carnival.

"Uh, Dad?" I said, putting my backpack down on the table.
He turned to me, surprised, and said, "Oh, hey, honey! Guess what?"
"What?" I went to him.

"I got a ticket for us to the Winter Wonderland Festival!"

"Really?" I wasn't really surprised. My dad is always into those wonderland and carnival things. He's more of an outdoors kind of guy, and I'm more of an indoors kind of girl. I only really do things inside.

A total difference between us—but I think I took that from Mom.

"Yeah!" he said happily. "And we're going today—in fact, *now!*"

"Oh, so… can I just go with these clothes?"

"Elle, these are the clothes you wear to school. You already know you can't take this outfit out—especially when we're going out to have fun!" He sighed dramatically.

"Okay, okay, I'll go change."

See what I mean? Intro—an introverted, lazy child. And it's totally from my mom.

CHAPTER 9

When we came back home, I actually didn't want to come back. The place was totally fun! I wasn't expecting the Wonderland thing to be so interesting and cool. I had to tell Marla about this. Now, I can finally say I had fun over break, even though school has already started.

"Marlaaa," I called out, flopping sideways across my bed with my phone resting on my cheek.

"Hey," she answered, her voice casual but curious.

"Guess where I just came from? The Winter Wonderland Festival!"

"No way! Isn't that like… your third one this season?" she replied, probably raising her brow.

I smirked. "Yeah, but this one hit different. They had a bunch of mini competitions—fifteen, I think? I only won two, but still!"

"Wait, what did you win?" she asked, probably already jealous.

I grabbed the plushie beside me. "A giant fluffy teddy bear, and this adorable pink Lululemon bottle."

There was a sharp gasp on the phone. "A Lululemon bottle and a teddy bear? Elle, I swear—you're living my dream. I'm literally jealous right now."

I laughed and twirled the bottle in my hand. "You can have the bear if you want. I've got like a zoo of plushies already. He'll just get lost in the crowd."

"For real? That's actually so sweet. Bring it to school tomorrow, okay?"

"You got it," I said, already placing it by my bag.

"Love you, bye, Elle," she sang.

I grinned and hung up.

But before I could turn off my phone, I saw a missed call from PrinceTrev. I didn't want to call, so we just texted:

Hi, I typed.

Hey, how've you been? You didn't answer my calls, he said.

Oh, I went to this festive Wonderland thing, and it was pretty cool, honestly.

Ah, nice. So… are you free to play a round of MS Car Racing? he typed in less than five seconds.

Um, I don't think so. I have school tomorrow, sorry.

Oh, it's okay. But are you free tomorrow, though?

I paused for a minute before typing: Yeah, maybe. But I'll try texting you, and we could play a round.

Okay, sounds cool. Good night, Els.

Good night.

CHAPTER 10

The next day at school, Marla was sick, so she couldn't come. Now I was wondering who I'd sit with at lunch—and I still had to give her the fluffy bear I got from the competition. But right after I thought about it, I heard my name yelled out behind me. I turned, and it was Travis.

"Oh, hey," I said with a small wave.

"Hi," he replied, flashing a crooked smile.

"You really walked from the main doors just to say hi to me?"

He scratched the back of his neck, shifting his weight. "Maybe I did… maybe I didn't. I don't know—guess I just ended up here."

I let out a chuckle, already amused.

Then he glanced around before asking, "Would it be cool if I hung out with you today? My friends have kind of been ignoring me since yesterday, and… well, you're the only person I actually feel like talking to right now."

I blinked. Travis—the new guy—wanted to spend the whole day with me. And the strange thing? I didn't even think about saying no.

"Alright, stay with me if you can." I shrugged with a smile.

"By the way, are you heading to class?"

"Yep, we can go together… milady."

"Milady?" Since when did this guy call me *milady*?

"No," he uttered, laughing. "You're milady, not me. I'm…
Travis."

I chuckled again. "Stop, you're gonna kill me with these jokes. Let's
just go to homeroom already."

In the first class, we had Math. I sat at a desk in the first row, in
the middle. There was an extra chair beside me, but I wasn't sure
anyone was going to sit there. As soon as I took out my books, though,
Travis came to sit beside me.

"Travis?" I said, confused and surprised that he was sitting near
me.

"Yeah?" he said, settling down.

"Why're you sitting here? I thought you'd be at the back or
something."

"Nah, I'm not the type of boy who's like the worst kids in the
class, always sitting in the back doing something weird."

"Wow, I guess you're way different from them?"

"Yeah. And you don't mind me—"

"Oh, it's okay, you can sit here."

I don't know why I was kinda blushing after that. It's pretty rare
to find me blushing at boys.

After school ended, I was walking home when I heard footsteps
behind me. I turned, and there was Travis. I waved at him and said,
"Hey."

He came closer, and I could smell the scent of his handsome
cologne.

"Hi," he smiled.

"If I may ask, why are you walking with me?" I uttered.

"My mom got a full shift at her workplace, so nowadays I have to walk home."

"What about your da—never mind… sorry."

"Oh, it's okay. But my dad lives really far from my house, that's why I usually just visit on weekends."

I just nodded and said nothing. It went quiet after that, but I didn't really like the silence, so I asked the stupidest, weirdest question—the kind I knew he'd probably say no to.

"Um… do you want to go to a coffee shop tomorrow to do the rest of the project?"

He sighed and chuckled oddly, and I braced myself for a "no."

"Sure. But we have a whole ten pages left to do, so I don't think we'll finish tomorrow."

"Oh, it's okay. Mrs. Jean said we have two more days before it's due."

"Great. So, I'll give you my number, and I'll text you when I'm going to the shop."

"Alright."

We shared our phone numbers, said goodbye, and went home.

It felt like my first time giving a boy my number to text or call— apart from the *Gameboy* in *MS Car Racing Gaming*. But I'll admit, I blushed really hard this time.

CHAPTER 11

Dear Diary, what if a normal French girl, who loves boyish games and kind of has a boyish personality, has a big crush on a cute, tall French boy? Well... as simple as it—and obvious—it's me. I just can't stop loving how funny, kind, and smart he is. But today, I'm gonna confess my feelings to him—to Travis.

We're going to the coffee shop, and I know it's a little too early for that since we've only hung out for about two days, but... I have to. I'm bold enough to tell him anyway.

I informed my dad that I was going to the coffee shop to finish my school project, and when he heard me say a *boy* was doing it with me, it felt like he was going to disagree.

"Wait, what do you mean a boy is doing it with you? Is he your classmate?" he asked, confused.

"Yeah," I replied, lacing my shoes. "Travis, the new kid—remember him? We're partners for the project."

"Yes, but why can't you just do it at school? Do you really have to go to a coffee shop to finish it?"

I knew Dad could trust Travis. I hadn't really told him about him, but from the looks he gave me on the assistant-thing day, he kind of found him cool—like me.

"Yes, Dad, don't worry. I'll be back before you know it. Love you, bye!"

I quickly vanished out of the house before he could say or ask anything.

When I arrived, I saw Travis in the shop and waved.

"Hey," I said, sitting beside him.

"Hi. Did you bring the stuff?"

"Yeah." I took out my notebook, pen, pencil, and the physics book.

We didn't say anything after that and went straight to doing the project. Ever since Travis told me about the difference between our bottles, I've understood the project about mass and gravity more. After we wrote and studied about gravity and mass, we finally finished the project. I sighed loudly and rested on the chair.

"Ah, finally, we're done with this physics project," Travis uttered.

"Yeah, but I wasn't expecting it to be so hard," I said, looking at him.

"Eh, for me, it was kinda like learning about cats and dogs."

I chuckled. "Okay, funny guy, let's rest a little bit before going into jokes."

But actually, I didn't want to rest, because I just remembered the main reason why I came here—to tell him about my feelings for him. I sat up straight and changed my mood into a serious one.

"Uh, Travis… can I tell you something?"

He looked a bit confused when I said that. "Sure, what's up?"

"So, since you came to this school, I've realized how cool and nice you are—funny, especially. And—for some reason… I've started having—"

But right before I could finish my sentence, I got a call from my dad. I didn't really want to answer, but then I got texts from him saying, *'Elle, come home right now! I have big news to tell you.'*

Travis, who was hoping to hear my news with seriousness, asked, "What is it?"

I texted Dad that I'd be back home quickly, but that meant I couldn't tell Travis about my feelings. I packed my things and said goodbye to him. He waved back but looked confused—and I felt really bad.

Back at home, I opened the door to see a strange woman inside. She was chatting with my dad, and when they saw me, they looked surprised.

"What's going on?" I asked slowly, putting my things down on the floor.

"Uh…" Dad started. "Elle, meet Vanisha… your, your—"

"My what?" I got closer to them.

"Your mother."

Everything went quiet. I didn't know what to say. *My mother?* The woman whom I've never seen in my whole life, even since I was born? How is that possible? And after all these years—now she's back?

"What—where have you been all this time?" I asked, shocked, looking at my mother.

"Well, my family and I have been having serious problems, and when they found out I was pregnant with you, they didn't allow me to take care of you well. That's why you've never seen me since birth," she said, trying to make me understand.

But I didn't say anything, mostly because I was confused.

"And I'm sorry," she said, looking dejected. "I'm sorry I've ignored you since. Your dad didn't want any issues with you and me if we met."

"Wait, so you guys are not divorced or anything?" I asked.

"No, we used to talk when you were younger, but then we stopped and lost touch. We didn't want our problems to interfere with your life as you grew up," Dad uttered.

He then came closer to me, holding my palm. "I wanted to take care of you fully, so I put your mom aside. And I promise you, we understand whatever good or bad feelings you have about this."

What I felt was like crying a little bit. I was the only person in my family—whether my mom's or not—who had never been raised by a mother. I was kind of glad my mother was finally home, though. It may sound weird, but some kids would still disagree and not accept their "back home parent." But not me—I always give people second chances.

And it wasn't like my parents were divorced; they just had to take a break for a bit, since my mother had some serious problems to solve with her family. And my dad wanted what's best for me—to care for me. Honestly, I kinda understood the disruption.

"Well... I'm a bit shocked to say that I missed you." I chuckled under my breath.

My mother wrapped her arms around me. "Me too, Elle, and I always thought about you when I was away."

"Please don't leave me again, then." I stared at her dark forest-green eyes.

She pulled back, gently stroking my cheek. "I won't. It's a promise."

So, after hanging out a little with my (reunited) parents, I remembered I still hadn't told Travis my feelings, so I went upstairs to my room and called him. It took a while before he answered.

"Hi," I said.

"Hey," he muttered, sounding like a dull, unbothered guy.

"Look, I'm sorry I had to go last minute. My family needed to tell me some big news." I fidgeted with my fingertips.

"It's alright, but... weren't you about to say something before you left?"

I stammered. "Uh..."

"Something about me. What was it?"

I took a deep breath and hoped he wouldn't reject me after I brought out my feelings.

"Well, lately... I've been having feelings for you, and it's mostly about how funny and smart you are. But I'm really hoping you won't reject me."

I heard him chuckle, and I knew it was the end for me.

"Elle... you know, I've also been having feelings for you."

I was staggered. "Wait, really?"

"Yeah, but it wasn't because of your personality or anything. It was because I had a feeling you were the same *'Els'* from the MS Car game."

Uh-oh.

"Is it really you, though?" he asked.

"Um… yeah. But how'd you find out?" I rubbed my neck.

"Well, *Els* sounded exactly like your real name—*Elle*—and when you told me you play car racing games, I put two and two together and found out."

Whoa… he's so smart he even found out about me. And I'm very dumb, because how the heck did I also think of making my fake name sound exactly like my real name?!

"So… you're the *PrinceTrev* guy?"

"Yep." He made a dramatic sigh.

Now, Diary, don't think this is weird, but in case I have kids in the future and they ask me how I met my boyfriend, I'd say it was a very wonderful and shocking moment—mostly because we both like the same thing (racing games), and we have feelings for each other. But that's not going to happen unless we marry, of course.

"Um… now that that's over, want to play some rounds of *MS Car Racing*?" I asked, relieved.

"Sure, milady."

I'm sure later in the future, he'll be calling me *milady* and other cute names that I'd admire.

And so, Diary, that's the end of my story—about how my family separated and reunited, and also how a young, funny, smart guy and I fell in love with each other.

SO...THAT WAS FRIENDSHIP?

"Not every goodbye is spoken."

CHAPTER 1

Everyone says Grade 8 is supposed to be your year. For Charlie Davins, it's a mix of excitement and nerves. It's not a new school, thankfully, but the class won't be the same. Some old classmates might be there, but with new people coming in, fitting in feels like a big question mark.

Anyway, I was in my room, lying back on my bed, staring at the ceiling, chewing on the end of my pencil. My notebook was open beside me, half filled with random to-do lists, crossed-out ideas, and a heading that read:

"Grade 8 Plan" (with three question marks).

"S.M.," I said.

S.M. is just short for "school makeover." It involves doing new things and getting ready for a new year at school. But it's really hard to make one—especially when you don't have someone to do it with you.

"That's it!" Then I realized I could call my friends to help me with it. I grabbed my phone and tapped Madelyn's name. She's my first-ever best friend—who has the same birthday and last name initial. The phone rang twice.

"Heyyy," she answered, dragging out the *y* like she always did when she was bored.

"Hey," I said, already feeling calmer. "What are you doing?"

"Lying on my couch. Half-watching a show I've already seen. Why?"

I sat up. "Okay, don't get annoyed... but I need your help."

"With what?"

"Planning. Like, getting everything together before school starts. The S.M. For us. Like last year—just... not a disaster this time."

There was a pause. I could hear her shifting, probably grabbing a bag of chips or something.

"You called me... for life planning?"

"Yes," I said. "School starts next week, and I feel like I'm walking into a war zone without armor."

She snorted. "You're so dramatic."

"Not dramatic. Realistic. We need outfit opinions. Hair advice. A full-on rebuild."

"Wow. Okay," she said, fake-serious. "So we're scrapping the old Charlie and building a better one?"

"Not just me—all of us. The three of us. If we're doing Grade 8, we're doing it right this time."

"Well... I still think last year worked," she said. "You just need to try again. Maybe this time you'll succeed."

"What does this have to do with success?" I groaned. "Madi, come on. Please. Can we just make a real plan this time?"

She was quiet for a second. "Fine. But next year—no S.M."

"Yes! Okay, please call Elisha when you're coming."

"Bye," she said with a grumpy attitude.

I tossed my phone on the bed and ran downstairs to wait. Eliott—my brother—was on the couch, locked into some anime movie. I grabbed a squishy toy from the old armchair and tossed it at him.

"Man, don't you love anime so much? Might as well marry it!"

He blinked at me, confused. "What?"

"Whatever," I said, rolling my eyes. "Wait—where's Mom?"

"Uh... probably in the backyard with Dad," he mumbled, eyes still glued to the screen.

I sat on the last stair, drumming my fingers against the railing. Ten minutes later, the doorbell finally rang. I opened it with a grin.

"Hi! Welcome. And ignore the anime lover over there," I said, pointing at Eliott.

"I am not an anime lover! And it's *otaku*!" he yelled from the couch.

"Shut up!" I crossed my arms.

"So," I said, turning back to my friends, "room or dinner table?"

"Room," Elisha answered, already kicking off her shoes.

I grabbed their sneakers and tucked them neatly onto the shelf. Grade 8 planning was officially in session.

CHAPTER 2

In my room, we were thinking about what to do for the S.M. Elisha took a sheet of paper and started writing.

"What are you doing?" I asked.

"Oh, I'm making a checklist," Elisha said, focusing on her writing.

"What checklist?" Madelyn asked, confused.

"It's called *'Fabulous Things to Do Before We Start Grade 8.'*"

"Oh, wow," I said, raising my eyebrows.

"That's—" Madelyn started but got interrupted by Elisha.

"Amazing! Right?"

"Uh, yeah. That was definitely what I was about to say," Madelyn chuckled, rubbing her neck.

"If you don't like it, then just say it—" Elisha sighed, already crumpling the paper.

I stopped her. "No! I like it—in fact, I love it. I think this will make our S.M. perfect!"

"Uh, yeah, it's great, Elisha," Madelyn added in a mutter.

Madelyn's the kind of girl who genuinely enjoys lying—like, she finds it fun. But deep down, she knows it messes with people's feelings. Elisha, on the other hand, gets hurt way too easily. One offhand comment and she's replaying it in her head for a week. They've known each other forever, but when it comes to emotions, it's like they forget how close they are—like strangers avoiding the truth.

I pinched Madelyn's elbow and frowned for a second.

"Okay, let's start," I said, clearing my throat and looking over Elisha's checklist.

We started thinking of ideas, but it was really hard because, c'mon— we're finally seniors. We're going to be the big girls next week. Very soon, we'll be going to parties alone, at night! Crazy, right? So we had to think of amazing ideas—like getting money or getting makeup.

After we made our list (which took us half an hour), we finally had a fabulous checklist for Grade 8. This was the list:

1. Get detention
2. Do something we know we'll hate
3. Help humanity
4. Make a guy friend (not a *boyfriend*)
5. Highlight our hair

"Wow, I think this list might help us survive Grade 8," Madelyn said, looking boldly at the list.

"Heck yeah, it's gonna! Then why in the world would we even sign up for this?" Elisha said.

"I mean, it must help us, because if it doesn't, we'll be doomed," I said, looking worried.

"And also be embarrassed," Madelyn added.

"Oh, c'mon, guys! We took about an hour to think and think about what would help us for Grade 8, and this is your reaction?" Elisha said, twisting her head toward us as her round glasses twitched.

"I don't know, maybe this was a bad idea. We should probably use the YouTube way." I hated saying that, but I wanted to anyway.

"Really, Charls? This was your idea in the first place! And I know you're nervous, but this is the only way to help solve the S.M. thing."

"I guess she's right," Madelyn said, looking at me with her deep, mossy eyes.

"Great! Now, c'mon—I'm starving. Do you have any crackers or something?" Elisha stretched and put the checklist away.

"Uh, yeah. I do," I said, getting up.

We immediately started discussing what to do first over the weekend after finishing our snacks from the new groceries Mom had bought for me and Eliott.

Madelyn, eating her last cream cracker, said, "Oh! What about... highlighting our hair first? Because, you know, it's kind of something you have to do before school. And besides, my mom always wanted me to do my hair, so I think we can try to get our parents to accept it. What do you think?"

"I think... that's a great idea! My mom will definitely allow me," Elisha said.

They turned to each other and started whispering funny jokes about how easily their parents would let them do their own hair.

And that's another thing about my friends—they never tend to think about my opinion.

"What about me? My mom will for sure not allow me. You know how she is. How about... 'Help Humanity'? It's better, because then everyone will know how kind we are!" I said with no enthusiasm, cutting into their private conversation.

"Really, Charlie? C'mon, now you're being the introvert one here. You gotta be brave for school this term," Elisha uttered.

"Yeah, and again, you're the one who brought this thing up anyway. Don't worry—we'll help you get your mom to understand," Madelyn said, trying to convince me.

"Ugh, fine. But if this does *not* work, we stop, alright?"

"Alright, alright," Madelyn said with a dull attitude.

I felt a little awkward and, honestly, confused with myself for even thinking this whole plan might not work. But they were right—the plan should be good. I mean... I'm the one who thought of it.

"Okay, you guys have to go now. I need to do my laundry, and I don't think you'd like to watch me do that," I said to them.

"Yeah, bye, Charls!" Elisha tossed her big bag of chips into my pink Hello Kitty trash can and headed out.

"See you tomorrow," Madelyn said, following her.

CHAPTER 3

The next morning, I went downstairs to see Mom and Dad fighting in the kitchen. I didn't want to interrupt, but I also didn't like what they were doing. Nowadays, they fight a lot, but since my brother and I are kind of used to it, we don't really complain—unless it's in front of our friends or when we're doing something serious.

I asked, "Um, Mom, Dad... what's going on?"

Mom turned to me and said, "Oh, honey, nothing is going on. We're just... just—"

Dad gave Mom a look that clearly meant *Get it together* before saying, "Just talking about financial problems."

"Yeah, financial problems. What do you need?" Mom said, clearing her throat.

"Uh, I just wanted to see if there's breakfast," I mumbled.

"Oh, right." Mom took a plate and dished out my food from the pan on the stove.

"Mmm, eggs and waffles. Thanks, Mom!"

After I finished, I went back up to my room. But I still wondered what they were talking about, because I knew they weren't talking about *financial problems.* So I tried to listen through the wall, but... all I could hear was yelling—and something about a... relationship?

I didn't really hear what they were saying, so I just got changed into my favorite summer floral dress and called my best friends.

When they came, we went back to talking about the hair highlights. Madelyn sat on my gaming chair and said, "So, I was thinking—maybe just the ends of our hair? Because we don't wanna dye our whole hair, ya know?"

"Yeah, I think that's a good idea," Elisha said with a shrug.

"Okay, so now all we have to do is tell our moms," I stated.

"Well, we already told our moms…" Madelyn muttered.

"Oh. I guess I have to tell my mom now," I said, scratching my hair awkwardly.

"You got this! I'm sure she'll say yes," Elisha said, putting her hand on my shoulder.

I then went to Mom's door and knocked. I entered and saw her on the bed, using her phone.

"Hey, Charls, what's up?"

"Uh, I need your permission for something."

"What is it?" She finally paused her typing and turned to me.

"So, my friends and I decided to make a list for Grade 8 this term. And…"

"And?" She got up and sat straight.

"And we wanted to highlight our hair first."

She went quiet for a while, and I knew she was going to say no.

"Um... today?"

"Yeah," I said, rubbing my neck as I felt the rough edge of my birthmark.

"Oh, honey, you know I can't allow that."

"But I'm thirteen! You have to—at least just this once," I pleaded, moving closer and touching her hand. "Please, just today, this year, for school."

"... Fine."

"Really? Yes! Thanks, Mom, I love you so much!"

"Alright, but only highlighting—not dye, not haircut. Just highlights, okay?"

"Mhm." I nodded with a grin.

"And if you're going tonight, you must be here by... six p.m.," she said, checking her phone.

"Okay, thanks, Mom!"

I was so happy she finally said yes to something I really wanted. I went back to my room and gave a big smile to make my BFFs realize my mom had said yes too.

Elisha jumped up, clapping her hands. "Ooh, I knew she would agree!"

"Now all we have to do is go to the salon, pay, and do our hair!" Madelyn said, smiling.

"Yeah. But who's taking us? I mean, both of your parents are working, and we also can't go alone—it's way too far!" I said.

"What about your mom?" Elisha asked.

"Oh, I don't know... she seems tired, and I think she'll be going to work any minute."

"Then she could just drop us there. We could take a bus back—or call my dad to bring us back since he finishes work late," Madelyn suggested.

"Oh, that's a good idea," I said.

"Great! Let's go," Elisha said, grabbing her phone.

When we reached, we walked in—and boy, was the place packed! About fourteen people and four hairstylists were there.

"I guess we won't finish soon," Elisha said, looking around.

I went to the counter and booked a service. The lady at the desk told us we'd be called in about fifteen minutes.

"Fifteen minutes?!" Madelyn exclaimed.

"We won't even be done by seven p.m.," Elisha added.

"It's fine, guys. Let's just wait in the waiting room," I said.

After waiting and waiting, it was finally our turn. While we were getting our hair done, I could see in the mirror that the hairstylists were only working on the ends of our hair. Then they washed and dried it—and after all that work, it was done. Our hair looked *so* beautiful! I loved it.

"Wow, this is some really good makeover," Madelyn said, touching her hair.

"Yeah," Elisha said, surprised.

My hair was light yellow at the ends, Elisha's was light pink, and Madelyn's was light blue.

When we finished paying and everything, Madelyn called her dad to pick us up.

When we all got home, I went straight to my room and checked off *'Highlight hair'* on the list.

"This is going so great!" I said, smiling softly to myself.

CHAPTER 4

The next day, after breakfast and doing my chores, I called my friends and told them to come right away, like it were an emergency. And while I was waiting for them, I saw Mom crying in the kitchen.

I went to her and asked, "Mom, what's wrong?"
She started crying more, and I didn't really like that. It was kind of embarrassing.

She finally answered, "Oh, nothing. Just... adjusting to some bad news."

"What bad news? Is it really that bad?"
Gosh, why did I ask that? It was stupid. Isn't it obvious enough that it was bad?

She stopped crying and looked down at the countertop.
"It's not something you should be worried about, Charls. But thanks for your concern."

I worry about my mom sometimes. She and Dad have been fighting for a long time, and Eliott hasn't been doing anything to help. He doesn't even seem to care. Well, I do. But my parents won't tell me what's going on. I try to find out sometimes, but I think they have their reasons why.

Anyway, when the girls arrived, we went to my room and started to pick something else from the list to do for Grade 8. Madelyn took one of my red ballpoint pens and started spinning it between her fingers.

"Man, I can't believe we pulled this off," she said.

"Yep. Isn't it amazing?" Elisha nodded, looking around my room.

I then took the checklist and got an idea.

"Guys, what about 'help humanity' now?"

"Ooh! That's a good one," Elisha uttered.

We all then decided to help at the Elder Community Service Apartment. Since we got permission from our parents, we walked to the place. When we arrived, I found a patient to assist at the service. We went upstairs and knocked on the door.

It took him a good two minutes before yelling, "What?!"

I cleared my throat. "Uh, sir, we're part of the service team. We're just here to help clean your room and, um… offer advice?"

The door creaked open, and the old man looked us up and down, completely confused.

"Who are you?"

"Service helpers?" Elisha mumbled, already regretting it.

"You look like ten–year–olds!"

"We're actually thirteen," I corrected, like that somehow helped.

"Well, I'm still not letting thirteen–year–olds clean my house!"

Then he slammed the door.

"Looks like we have a hard one," Madelyn sighed.

I looked at his paper chart, and his name was Frank Williams. He was a retired Olympic coach.

I knocked on his door again and said, "Um, Mr. Frank, please. I know you don't like this—especially us entering your room—but we also don't. So let's just hurry this up and get this done."

"Fast," Madelyn added.

It went quiet, and then I heard a click on the doorknob. I knew he'd unlocked the door. We slowly entered, and his room looked kinda… messy.

"Oh boy, this is going to be some frustrating work," Elisha murmured.

We started in the bedroom. I worked on his desk, which honestly wasn't too messy—except for the moldy dark curtains that were supposed to be white. They kept distracting me every time my arm brushed against them.

When I turned to my right, Madelyn was in the closet, cleaning while pinching her nose so hard I thought she might faint any second from the horrible, damp smell coming off his musty socks and clothes, which, again, were also supposed to be white.

Elisha didn't do much, though. She just swept the floor, but even then, she had trouble vacuuming because the machine was clogged with heavy debris.

We finally did the last part of the house—the living room—and Mr. Frank was watching the news.

I asked, "What are you watching over there, Mr. Frank?"

"The Olympics," he answered back.

"Oh, you also like the games of the Olympics?"

He turned to me and said, "Yes. In fact, I used to be in it."

"Really?" I stopped cleaning the dining table.

"Yep. I was one of the best competitors—and a coach. Boy, do I wish I could go back into the past."

He looked up, pretending to imagine his younger self.

"Oh, wow. So you actually retired then?"

"Of course! Look at me, I'm fifty-five years old. I can't play anymore."

"Well, I'm sure you still know some moves, right?"

"Uh, yes. But I can't do them because I'm old—how many times do I have to tell you? Can't you hear well?!"

My voice went low. "Sorry, I didn't mean it."

When we finished cleaning, we tried to advise Mr. Frank on some tips to prevent his apartment from getting dirty quickly. But he wouldn't listen.

"It's just a little information. I know you don't want dirt in your room," I said to him.

"What? I am not taking advice from thirteen–year–olds!"

"C'mon, sir. I know you don't like it and don't want us here, so please, let's just get this over with. I promise it'll help you," Elisha muttered.

"And there's nothing wrong with thirteen–year–olds advising elderly people," Madelyn added, crossing her arms.

"… Fine. But make it quick," Mr. Frank said, looking annoyed.

After all that dramatic scene, we walked back home.

"Gosh, that was such a terrible service," Elisha said, panting.

"Yeah, and I didn't know elderly people are like that," Madelyn said.

"Well, that didn't go well at all. And Mr. Frank is not just a regular problem person."

"Mhm, and I didn't know a guy like him was in the Olympics?" Elisha said, confused.

"Didn't you see the medals and trophies on the table?" Madelyn said to Elisha, scoffing in surprise.

CHAPTER 5

The next morning, while I was doing my chores downstairs, Mom came from her room all smiley.

"So, Charlie, I was thinking—maybe we could go out today. We could go to that 'Swiss Chalet' restaurant you always wanted to visit, and while we're at it, you could buy some stuff for school tomorrow at the mall. Hmm?"

I was a little bit surprised. I mean, this week, she and Dad kept on fighting, and she'd been sad all day. So it was really weird—and unusual—that she was giving me this favor.

But I was still pleased. "Um, okay, that's great! I'd love to."

"OK. After you finish your chores, go get ready, and then we can go."

After I finished my shower, I decided to go for a more mature, teenage look. I was definitely channeling the vibe of my favorite influencer, Emma Chamberlain. I parted my hair into two sections and styled it in its naturally wavy texture—it always curled up whenever I scrunched it.

My outfit leaned more grown–up this time: a basic, fitted white tee paired with light blue, flared pants. The lace–up ankle boots were from Zara and totally pulled the whole look together.

After that, we got into the car. Mom kept smiling to herself, like she knew something I didn't—and honestly, it was starting to weird me out.

I asked, "Mom? What's with your smiling face today?"

"Oh, just me being in a happy mood!"

"Really? I thought you were still fighting with Dad?"

Mom then frowned and changed the subject.

"So, how was the community service yesterday?"

"Uh, we had this elderly patient, and he was so rude. Like, he's not that type of cool and chill elderly person you'd expect to find. His name was Frank Williams—but I think his name should be *Mr. Strictly Williams* instead."

"Oh, I guess it wasn't good after all," she said, frowning, surprised by what I said.

When we were in the mall getting things for school, I saw two girls who looked exactly like Madelyn and Elisha.

Mom looked at them and asked, confused, "Wait, aren't those your friends?"

It *was* them. I went a little closer to inspect and saw one of the girls' hair, and that was definitely Elisha's light–pink hair.

"What are they doing here?" I asked, bewildered.

I also saw another girl between them. They were all giggling and having fun. But didn't they tell me they both still had one day of summer school?

And they were also buying school stuff. I thought they had already bought theirs last week. Were they lying?

Mom wanted to talk to them and their parents, but I resisted. I mean, wouldn't it be embarrassing to see both of us shopping at the same mall, buying the same things for school—when some of us shouldn't even be there?

At home, while we were having dinner, Mom kept looking at me weirdly. Smiling, actually—just like this morning.

I looked back at her and asked, "Mom, why are you looking at me like that again?"

"Oh, just accepting the fact that we saw your friends at the mall, they said they *hate*—and another girl laughing with them."

"So? That was probably another friend. I can't be the only one. And besides, they didn't say *hate*—they said *dislike*. No problem."

Then Eliott started looking at me even more weirdly.

"Ugh, what now?" I said, annoyed.

"Are you jealous?"

"What? No!" I slammed the fork back onto the plate.

In my room, I tried texting my friends about today's coincidence, but what if they said I couldn't trust them because I had seen them with another girl?

Although they lied to me.

But Eliott was right. I *was* jealous. Like—why wouldn't I be? They lied to me, and they don't even like that mall!

At one point, I tried calling them about three times, but they didn't pick up. I just needed to see and chat with them one more time before school starts tomorrow.

But even on Snapchat—the place they're *mostly* online—they still didn't pick up.

I didn't know if it was pretend... or just to annoy me.

CHAPTER 6

Today was my first day at school. I was finally going to Grade 8, and I was a senior. I was really nervous at first, but as I entered and saw the same classes, teachers, and kids, I knew I wouldn't suffer. The class would start in ten minutes, so I tried waiting for my best friends, but... I didn't see them.

Until I saw three girls walking to the entrance, laughing and wearing matching outfits. I was really shocked to see my friends—sorry, *"best friends"*—talking to the same girl from yesterday.

I went up to them and said, "Hey!" Not in a rude way, though.

Elisha turned to me and said, "Oh, hey, Charlie! Meet Aria."

"Our other friend," Madelyn added.

"Hi!" Aria smiled.

"Friend?" I asked.

"Yes, any problem with that?" Elisha asked, confused.

"No! I mean, I didn't know you guys had another friend, and you never told me," I said.

"Oh, well, sorry about that. We never had the time," Elisha uttered, chuckling in Aria's ear.

"You could have called or texted me?" I said, crossing my arms.

"Does it really matter? You've already met her, so..." Madelyn said, annoyed.

In Literacy class, I could hear my friends talking at the back—and it was about boys. But they said they hated boys. Especially when it came to crushes, they wouldn't even insist. I really wanted to get out of there because the noise was distracting me.

I didn't want to tell on them, but… there was no choice. Either I listened to them talk about something they said they hated, or I told the teacher and moved somewhere else so I could focus and understand the lesson.

So I raised my hand and said, "Um, Miss Chino?"

"Yes?" She paused at the board.

"I'm getting distracted by the noise at the back. Can I please move somewhere else?"

"Why, sure! Sit beside Mark, please."

I was pleased that there was no noise where I was sitting now, but the girls were looking at me like I hated them for talking.

In the next class, Biology, I was sitting beside the same boy from the first period. It seemed he was actually the new kid in our homeroom. And he didn't look or act bad, unlike the other guys, who I should really call little kids, because their whole title and personality were just childish.

He looked at me and said, "Hey."

"Hi," I said back.

"I'm Mark."

"I know. I was sitting beside you in the first class," I chuckled softly.

"Oh, yeah. I know."

"Well, I'm Charlie—but people call me Charls."

"Oh, nice. I actually thought the name Charlie was meant for boys."

"Really?" I tilted my head, getting a bit interested.

"Yeah! And honestly, I marked it in my notebook—'Names for Boys.'"

I didn't know if what he said was *that* funny, but I couldn't hold back my laugh—it slipped out louder than I meant, and a few heads turned. He had a really good sense of humor—the kind of person you don't get tired of talking to. I had a feeling we'd get along well.

At home, Mom and Dad were still arguing, but this time it escalated. Dad raised his hand like he was about to hit her, and without even thinking, I stepped in. I grabbed his arm and pushed it back before he could do anything.

My voice shook as I said, "Dad, what are you doing?"

He froze, completely stunned—like even he couldn't believe what just happened. "Uh, I… I—"

"Did you just try to hit Mom?" My voice was breaking down. I didn't want to cry, but… I could see Mom's tears dripping down.

Mom then turned to me and said, "Oh, honey, he was just… about to wipe my tears. Yeah… tears."

"Wipe your tears? Mom, why do you keep lying to me? First, I hear you guys talking about a *financial problem,* and then you tell me 'nothing is going on.' But I know something is going on—I know it! And you better tell me before it gets too late!"

I stormed off to my room, shut off the lights, and called my best friends. None of them picked up. I tried texting again and again, but still no reply.

That's when I realized something was off with them, too—something I wasn't part of.

CHAPTER 7

The next day at school, I was sitting with Mark again. Clearly, my best friends hadn't really been talking to me. They'd been whispering behind my back more than usual, and this time, they weren't even trying to be quiet. I could clearly hear them laughing about random things—like someone's mom being overly affectionate in public—and, of course, Aria was right in the middle of it.

The teacher saw them and said, "Okay, girls at the back—that's enough. You can see I'm teaching, and you're talking? And this is the second time."

Madelyn, pretending to feel sorry, said, "We're sorry." But everyone knew she was lying.

"No, you're getting detention."

"What?!" Elisha said, shocked.

"Now. Go."

I could tell they weren't happy about it, but… at least they filled one thing on the list—*getting detention.*

When school closed, I was walking home when I heard a familiar voice. I turned to see Mark running toward me.

"Oh, hey!" I said to him as he reached me.

"Hi, um… I was thinking, since clearly your parents didn't pick you up, maybe we could walk together?" He bent to his knees, panting for air.

"Isn't that weird?"

"Oh, I mean… if you don't want to—"

"I was just joking, silly! Of course, we can walk together," I chuckled, patting his back softly.

"So, do you live around here?" I asked, looking at him.

"Uh, kind of. It's like six minutes to my house."

"Well, mine's like five minutes."

"Oh, okay. By the way, do you think those girls in class are like… sisters or something?"

I didn't know who he was talking about until he said *sisters.*

"Uh, you mean Madelyn, Elisha, and Aria?"

"Yeah, are they sisters?"

"Um, why are you asking me?"

I didn't want him to know that I was best friends with them. Then he'd think I was one of them—because some people in our class didn't really like them. And I just got him as a new friend. I couldn't lose him.

He looked confused and said, "Uh, I thought you guys were friends?"

"I mean, we are—well, *were*—until we stopped talking when school started. And they're not sisters; they're just friends. I was their friend too—best friend, technically—but… I don't think I am anymore."

Then we went quiet. We turned onto a street, and then he saw his house.

"Ah, that's my house right there."

"Wait—you also live around here?" I stared straight at his house, then at mine, which was at the corner.

"Um, yeah. You also do?"

"Yeah!"

"No way!" he chuckled softly.

"Mhm. I guess we have to go now."

"Um, before we go, is it possible I can get your number?"

I rubbed my neck and turned away. "Oh.. um, I don't know—"

"Oh, c'mon, I'd like to know you more. We could text or call?"

I froze for a second, not really expecting that. We'd only been talking for two days, and I was still trying to figure him out—figure *us* out, if there even was an *us*. But he didn't sound pushy; still, there was something in his voice that just sounded hopeful. I looked at him, trying to read more than what he was saying. Part of me hesitated, but another part didn't want to keep pushing people away right now.

"Yeah... okay," I said, unlocking my phone and typing the digits into his. He smiled when he saw it pop up, and for some reason, that made me smile too.

"'Kay, see you tomorrow!" he said, running to his house.

CHAPTER 8

The next morning, I walked into the dining room and saw my family already seated, their faces unusually quiet and serious. Something felt off, and I couldn't figure out why. Yesterday, they had this gentle happiness between them.

Mom looked up and gently told me to sit down. A few seconds later, Dad spoke, and what he said completely caught me off guard.

"I'm sorry, you two, but… your mom and I are getting a divorce."

He let out a heavy breath, his eyes barely meeting ours.

"What?" Eliott's voice cracked as he blinked rapidly, trying to make sense of it.

"I know this sounds sudden," Dad said, his voice low. "But we've thought about it for a while. It feels like the right thing now."

"Why?" I asked, barely above a whisper. My throat felt tight, and the room suddenly felt colder.

Mom finally spoke, her voice shaking. "We've been dealing with things we just… can't fix. There's been a lack of understanding, and honestly, we're not committed the way we used to be."

I stood up, my heart pounding. "And you're just telling us now? Like this?"

"Charls, we didn't plan it this way," Mom said quickly, her hands trembling. "We only made the decision last night."

Eliott stood too, his face red with anger. "And you're just okay with it? Just like that?" Without waiting for a response, he turned and stormed out of the house.

Mom reached for me gently. "I'm so sorry," she whispered through tears.

I stepped back. "No. Don't be sorry," I said, wiping my face as tears kept falling. "Because I already knew something like this was coming. You've been distant for months. I knew you'd hurt us—I just didn't know it would hurt this much."

I grabbed my bag and walked out, my chest aching, leaving behind a house full of silence, cracks, and things we couldn't fix.

When I reached school, I saw my friends at their lockers and ran up to them.

"Um… what's wrong?" Madelyn looked at me as if she had never seen me before.

"I–I just had to listen to the weirdest decision ever."

"What?" Elisha asked.

"My parents are having a divorce," I said, about to drop more tears from my reddish eyes again.

"Oh, really? Um…" Madelyn turned and rubbed her neck.

"What? Guys, I am shocked, sad, and worried! Who am I going to stay with now?!"

Aria looked at me like I was exaggerating.

"Guys!" I said, looking at them, confused.

"Look… Charlie, have you realized we don't really talk anymore?" Elisha asked.

"Uh, yeah. Isn't it weird?" I scoffed lightly, trying to make it sound odd.

"Well, it's because we don't like you anymore—especially this… 'Grade 8 Plan' thing."

My jaw dropped in shock when she said that. "What?"

"I'm really sorry, but I think we have to go our separate ways," Elisha continued.

"Oh, so you're ending our friendship because of the plan? And taking this… 'Aria', girl with you?" I raised my eyebrows, furrowing them afterward.

"Hey! She's a good friend. And besides, you're the reason why we are stressing out," Madelyn said.

"What do you mean?"

"Well, you've always been calling us every night, and we always come to your house—every day!" Elisha added.

"But you know why! You know I need your help!"

"Maybe get therapy?" Aria uttered.

I looked at her and gave an angry look. Then I said, "You're going to regret this. This isn't fair." And I walked away.

CHAPTER 9

After school, I walked home with Mark. This past week, he'd quietly become my emotional anchor—someone I could talk to without feeling judged. I appreciated him more than I let on, and honestly, he felt like the best friend I didn't know I needed.

He saw my face and realized I was down.

He asked, "What's wrong, Charls?"

"Oh, um… I just had a weird day. My parents are getting a divorce, and my friends were no help. Instead, they wanted to end our friendship—with just me out of the picture."

"Oh, I'm sorry. But I support you."

"Really? Why? You barely even know me."

"Yeah, but we're kind of friends, right? And now that I know what you're going through, I can't just leave—like how your friends did."

"Thanks. But I still can't believe they did that to me. Like, I thought we were best friends. But I guess not."

"Fake friends are a lot in this world. You don't expect it to be easy to find real friends out here."

"Yeah. Hey, at least I have you." I nudged his shoulder with a soft smile.

He chuckled under his breath. "Yeah. Me too."

I wasn't sure why, but there was this warmth rising in my face—and his too. We both felt it, even if we didn't say anything. It was a little unexpected, but there was something kind about it. Something real. I let the feeling go as we reached our street. Without another word, we turned to our homes.

The next day, I needed to do something—something that made a statement. Bold. Unapologetic. After everything they'd done, I wasn't just going to let it slide. This wasn't about revenge exactly... but I wanted them to feel a fraction of what they'd put me through.

After school, I sent a simple text asking them to meet me at the park. What they didn't know was that I'd brought my neighbor's bulldog, Hulk—huge, loud, and surprisingly obedient when he liked you.

A few minutes later, they showed up... with Aria. Of course, they did, as if they couldn't go anywhere without dragging her along. The second they spotted the dog, their faces dropped—and then came the screaming. I didn't even have to say anything. The look on their faces said enough.

Elisha climbed onto the ladder by the community center wall and yelled, "Charlie, what the heck is wrong with you?!"

"You know we hate dogs!" Madelyn added.

"Well, I told you you're going to regret this. Weren't you prepared?" I crossed my arms, and the harness on the dog tightened slightly.

"Prepared? If I knew, I wouldn't even have come anyway! Why did you do this? Just because of the friendship break?" Elisha said, coming down from the ladder slowly.

"It's not just because of that. It's also because you guys weren't there for me yesterday when I told you the bad news. And you replaced me with... Aria? I've never even seen her in this school!"

They went quiet, and I continued, "And right before school started, you had to ignore me on the last night? I called you guys that Sunday night, and you never picked up. So what's wrong with you?! Huh? What did I do to deserve this?"

"Your whole 'Grade 8 plan' and this divorce drama—it's tearing everything apart! We're tired of it, Charlie!" Madelyn snapped. "Sometimes, I honestly regret ever becoming friends with you."

"Oh, so this friendship was fake? Wow, you've really surprised me. But I guess I shouldn't be that worried. I have another friend, a good brother, and at least... my parents to support me for now. But you? I really hope I never see you guys again!"

Then I took the dog by the leash and walked off. I knew they were staring at me. It was for a good reason anyway.

UNDERNEATH IT ALL

"It's funny how the people you least expect…

end up being the ones who change

everything."

CHAPTER 1

I never thought I'd end up dancing with the one person I couldn't stand. Life's strange like that.

It's just me, my mom, and my older sister at home, though. My mom always says, "Jorelle's the quiet one—always thinking, never talking." And maybe she's right. Sometimes my Uncle Charlie drops by on weekends or breaks, usually with expensive gifts he tries to play off like they're no big deal. He's got money, but he doesn't act like it. Honestly, he feels more like a dad than the one who left. My real dad cheated and walked out on us. We don't talk about it much, but when we do… it still hits like it just happened.

That morning, I was halfway through getting ready when Mom's voice echoed from downstairs, calling for both me and my sister. I threw on a pair of fitted black tights, a clean white cropped top with a preppy edge, and some new socks before putting on my Converse. As I made my way down, the warm, sweet smell of pancakes, waffles, and hot chocolate drifted through the air. It wrapped around me like a soft hug—one of the few peaceful parts of my morning routine.

"I'm here!" I said, sitting down at the dark wooden table.

"Where's your sister?"

Before I could answer Mom, my sister, Jirelle, came downstairs wearing a crop top with a box-pleat skirt.

"Here," she said, adjusting her outfit and hair.

Mom looked at us briefly and said, "You sure you girls are comfortable wearing those… clothes?"

My sister and I exchanged confused looks, and I said, "Yeah, why ask?"

"Because you look… different," Mom said, pausing at some point in her words.

"What do you mean?" Jirelle asked curiously.

"Well… y'all are Black girls, so wearing… pleat skirts won't really suit you. And Jirelle, you normally wear oversized sweaters and baggy pants. Jorelle, you… well—"

"Mama, there's nothing wrong with what I'm wearing or what Jorelle's wearing. As long as we like it and it suits us, then it's fine. Also, us being Black doesn't mean we can't wear what we like," Jirelle snapped.

Now, when I said "snapped," I didn't mean Jirelle raised her voice at Mom. It's just that in our family, we're very honest people—even if it means being rude. As long as it's the truth, then it's a little bit okay. And Mom was kind of judging us, so Jirelle had to step in. She promised me when I was ten that anytime someone was being mean, she would defend me and protect me—even if it meant standing up to our own family.

But if you're thinking about my enemy, he's different from the usual bully. Jirelle has no business with me and would never have time to meet him in school for a pep talk or something.

"Okay, I'm sorry. I didn't mean it," Mom said.

Jirelle then took one of the pancakes on the table and said, "I'm also sorry I said that in a bad tone."

CHAPTER 2

After that… I don't know what to call morning. I met my friends on the way to school.

"So, anything happen over your weekend?" one of my friends, Tara, asked.

"Mm, not really. It was kind of boring, actually," I answered.

"Wait, Uncle Charlie didn't come this week?" She tilted her head.

"No. My mom said he was sick."

My other friend, Erika, declared, "Well, my weekend was great! I went to the airport to pick up my sister, who's been in New York for years! And—"

"OK, girl, we get it. You had the most awesome week ever," Tara chuckled.

We had History the second class—unfortunately, with the one teacher everyone dreaded: Mr. Clark. He's the kind of strict that doesn't just hover… it rules the whole room. He teaches both Math and History, which already says enough. He's been around for over a decade, so by now, we've all learned how to survive his intense, no-nonsense teaching style.

I was sitting at the side table with my best friends when he suddenly hit us with some news none of us saw coming.

"OK, class, I know school graduation is almost here."

The class made happy noises.

"—But we still need to do one more test… geometry shapes."

A boy at the back yelled, "What? Why?"

Mr. Clark replied, "Because the other classes have already finished their whole-year tests. And you guys haven't."

"Damn," Tara mumbled.

I wasn't all that surprised. I mean, it's not like we haven't had a million tests crammed into one month before. I saw it coming.

Mr. Clark told us we had about ten minutes left before the lunch bell, so we could "study" if we wanted. But let's be real—my class? Not exactly the quiet, focused type. About 30% were actually going over notes, and the rest? Doing literally anything else.

While I was studying with my best friends, a guy from my class walked over and said, "Sup, Hoopster."

It was Caleb—the most annoying guy on earth. Why? Because he's always messing with me. Teasing and bothering me… sometimes even straight-up bullying me. And honestly, there are days I swear I could strangle him to death.

He looked at me with those smug hazel eyes, and I gave him a death stare. "What do you want, Caleb?"

"Um, just saying hi?"

I glanced behind him. His little crew was already snickering and throwing him thumbs-ups.

"Hi, really?" I raised an eyebrow.

"What? I can't say hi to you now?"

Then, he stepped in closer. Like, way too close. I didn't want to give him the satisfaction, but his breath actually smelled… nice? Like cinnamon or something warm. For whatever reason, I leaned in a little too.

Big mistake.

Suddenly, cold, sticky slime landed on my head. It reeked. I froze. Caleb burst out laughing along with his friends.

And yeah—I almost cried partly because the smell was unbearable. But mostly? For a second, I genuinely thought he was about to hug me or something.

Caleb didn't say anything and just went back to his friends. I expected Mr. Clark to see the drama that just happened and send Caleb to the principal or something—but he didn't. He didn't even look in our direction. He avoided our faces and turned back to his desk.

I got up and headed to the door, but while I was walking out, Mr. Clark (finally) looked up and saw me.

"Whoa… you look and smell bad."

Wow. Thanks for the compliment.

"Excuse yourself to the bathroom, Jorelle."

Everyone turned to look at me, stunned. It was so embarrassing that I ran out of the class quickly and went straight to the bathroom.

CHAPTER 3

While I was in the bathroom trying to clean the disgusting, smelly slime off my head, Tara and Erika came to check up on me.

"Oh my God, are you okay?" Tara asked.

"Yeah, I mean, apart from the smelly thing on my head, I'm fine," I said as I removed one huge piece of the gooey slime stuck below my scalp.

"That guy is a savage beast!" Erika exclaimed. "I can't believe he did that to you. I mean, I know he's done some crazy pranks before, but this is too far!"

"Yeah, but I don't think that was just some random prank," Tara said as she gently picked slime out of my hair.

"It's fine, guys," I mumbled. "But… I actually thought he was gonna kiss me or something when he got that close."

Tara let out a half-laugh. "Maybe a hug, but a kiss? No way he'd kiss you."

I narrowed my eyes. "And why not?"

She hesitated, then said, "Well… one, you guys literally bully each other—everyone knows that. And two, I heard he doesn't even like Black girls."

Her words hit hard. I didn't even know what to say at first. Caleb and I had been in the same class for years. We basically grew up side by side—even if most of that time was spent fighting. We were actually close when we were younger. People used to joke about us being together, and back then, we didn't mind.

And Tara? She had a habit of twisting things to make them more dramatic than they actually were. So, I wasn't about to take her comment too seriously.

"Tara, I know he never said that," I said, quieter now. "I mean, yeah, I know he wouldn't want to kiss me—and I wouldn't either—but still… there was a chance. I was just saying… he could've."

Before she could respond, the bell rang, and just like that, it was time for lunch.

In the cafeteria, while we were eating at our usual table, two girls from our class, Mellie and Fay, walked over.

"Hey, Jorelle. How're you doing?" Fay asked.

I looked up, confused. "Um… I'm good. Why?"

Mellie, with dark brunette hair that reminded me of my mom's, leaned in slightly. "We saw what happened this morning in class."

"Yeah, and we just wanted to check if you're okay," Fay added.

I didn't answer—not because I was being rude, but because I genuinely didn't feel like going over it again. I didn't care to relive the moment, and honestly, I just wanted to forget about Caleb and his dumb little prank.

Thankfully, Tara spoke for me. "She's fine. There's no slime on her head anymore."

They nodded, slow and unsure, before walking off awkwardly.

That made me smile a little. "Thanks, Tara."

"You're welcome," she replied with a small grin, then took a bite of her sandwich like it was nothing.

CHAPTER 4

After lunch, we had gym. Our teacher, Coach Roberta, assigned us to practice our basketball skills. Most of the girls didn't want to and just went to the end of the gym to do TikTok dances. But not me — I was determined to practice my skills. Mama always wanted me to be a sports player. She sees me as a basketball or volleyball player.

Normally, because of my height. Almost all of the boys in my class were also tall, so I felt like a boy playing basketball. Erika played some rounds, but Tara decided to just sit on the bench and watch the game.

While I was playing, Caleb came beside me with the ball in his hands and said, "I didn't know you could play basketball… Hoopster."

I tried blocking him before he could make a shot. His friends kept yelling, "Bro, pass, pass!" He ignored them and continued, "Finished taking off the dirty slime from your head? That smells just like you."

I got so angry, and when the ball slipped from his hand, I took it and dribbled. But before he or someone else could block me, I made a quick, high bank shot. Tara got up and started applauding.

Then I shoved the ball into his hands and said, "Yeah, it actually wasn't so hard to clean — oh, and unlike you, I took a shower this morning. So maybe it's you who smells so bad."

Coach Roberta made me take a break and congratulated me. "Good shot, Jorelle. You could make a great basketball player, you know that?"

"Yeah, thanks, Coach," I said, then went back to the bench where Tara was sitting and drank some water. But while I was, Caleb kept staring at me with a serious look, like I had done something wrong. I barely cared; he deserved to be beaten by me.

At home, I was working quietly on my laptop when I heard the front door swing open. The air shifted. Mom came in, tense and worn. Behind her, Jirelle stormed in and dropped her backpack on the floor like it meant nothing.

"I just don't get why you won't buy it for me," she snapped, her voice already raised.

"Jirelle, please, calm down," Mama said, trying to steady herself.

I stood from my seat and turned, sensing the heaviness in the room. "What's going on?"

Mama began, "Your sister is upset over some clothes—"

"Some clothes?" Jirelle cut in. "Mama, this isn't just any outfit! It's the fit. The one everyone's wearing, the one that actually matters right now. And you're brushing it off like it's nothing?"

Mama's tone sharpened. "Jirelle, it's a hundred and ten dollars. You think I can just pull that kind of money from nowhere? It's not easy to make ends meet."

I stepped in, trying to make sense of it all. "So… Jirelle, you're asking for something really popular right now. And Mama, you're saying it's just too expensive?"

They both answered at once: "Yes."

Jirelle's voice rose again, more desperate than angry. "Mama, I know it's a lot. But you keep saying you'll get it eventually — and I don't want 'eventually' anymore. I want it now."

CHAPTER 5

Mama didn't respond. She simply turned away, climbed the stairs without another word, and closed her bedroom door behind her—hard.

I looked over at Jirelle, who was still standing in the same spot, breathing unevenly.

"That was... harsh," I said quietly.

She turned to me like I was someone she'd never seen before. "What?"

I hesitated. "Don't you think you were out of line?"

She stared at me, then, after a long pause, said, "Stay out of this, Jo. You don't get it."

And just like that, she disappeared upstairs too, her door echoing just like Mama's.

I stood alone in the hallway, unsure of what had just happened. Maybe she's right. Maybe I don't get it. But part of me thinks I do.

Jirelle used to be so determined, so full of plans. But ever since she lost that office job, she hasn't moved forward. No new applications, no college forms, no next step. That job gave her money, yes—but it also gave her purpose. Without it, she's been drifting, clinging to whatever makes her feel in control.

And Mama... she's doing the best she can. There are bills, responsibilities, and worries she never talks about. I get both sides. I really do. But between reason and emotion, silence often wins.

And tonight, it did.

CHAPTER 6

Today at school, we had big news. We went to the gym and waited for the announcements.

Our principal, Mrs. Wilkinson, stepped onto the stage and addressed the crowd. "Good morning, staff and students. As you all know, graduation is just around the corner."

The gym buzzed with quiet agreement. She smiled and said, "To celebrate, your teachers and I have planned a *Paradise Dance* for the entire school!"

Cheers and applause erupted instantly.

Most were excited about a dance party on graduation day, but honestly, I wasn't thrilled. Why? Because I don't really know how to dance—well, except for that one silly move I picked up as a kid, but that doesn't count.

Mrs. Wilkinson went on, "There's a twist, though. Kindergarteners will have a pizza and dance party in the morning. Elementary students, in Grades 1 through 5, will participate in a costume-themed dance party. And the middle schoolers, Grades 6 through 8, will have a *date dance party*."

Some kids were disappointed they wouldn't get pizza like the little ones, while others were excited about the chance to dance with their crush.

But back in our math class, while Mr. Clark was handing out our test, a boy got up from his chair and interrupted the class.

"Uh, excuse me, everyone, but I want to ask a special person a question."

We all turned to him, wondering who he was talking about.

Mr. Clark looked annoyed and said, "Josh, please, sit."

Josh ignored him, looked at the girl with curly blonde hair in the front—who always wore lots of jewelry—and asked, "Brenda, will you go on a date with me to the dance party?"

Everyone was shocked and started hitting their tables, chanting, "Say yes! Say yes!"

Brenda looked really surprised and was blushing like crazy. I honestly hoped she would say yes.

It took about a minute, but she finally said, "Yes, I will."

Almost everyone got up and applauded them. Josh went to her and hugged her. But Mr. Clark looked angry—like he was about to rage. I guess he didn't like the "date party" idea. He firmly instructed everyone to sit and continued handing out the math tests.

After class, I was walking in the hallway to the cafeteria for lunch when my best friends came up to me.

"Hey, Jo!" Tara said, touching my shoulder.

"Hi."

They kept smiling at me like I'd sacrificed myself for them or something.

"What?" I asked, confused.

Erika touched my shoulder too and said, "Who's your date?"

Ohh, now I knew what this was about.

"Date?" I asked. "What date? I don't have a date."

"Girl, I know you do. C'mon, I bet there's this guy you like who you want to go with to the party," Tara smirked.

And for some reason, I stammered, "No, I... I don't even have a crush!"

That's when Caleb passed by us with his friends and said, "Sup, Hoopster."

Tara turned back to me. "Oh, really?"

I hit my forehead gently in disbelief. They really thought Caleb was my crush. "Look, he is *not* my crush!"

In the cafeteria, while we were all waiting for lunch, I noticed Caleb sitting just one table away. He kept glancing over at me, and it was starting to mess with my head. Eventually, I looked back at him— and then we just... kept staring.

Neither of us said a word, but there was something about it. As weird as it sounds, I think I kind of liked it.

CHAPTER 7

After school, I was walking home alone when I heard footsteps approaching behind me. I turned, and there he was—Caleb—catching up quickly. Maybe he wasn't coming toward me... or maybe he was. I slowed to a stop.

"Hey," he said. So yeah, he definitely was.

"Hi," I replied. Somehow, we ended up walking side by side. "Can I ask, why exactly are you walking with me?"

"Can't I?" he shot back, a little too casually.

"Well, yes—I mean, no. Actually, I—"

"Okay, okay, I get it. Relax." He chuckled.

I rubbed the back of my neck, trying to hide the warmth rising in my cheeks.

Then he said, "So, what's going on with you, Hoopster?"

I groaned. "Can you stop calling me that?"

"Calling you what?" he asked, like he genuinely didn't know.

"You know what I mean. Every time you come around, it's 'Sup, Hoopster' this, or 'How you doing, Hoopster' that."

"I thought you liked it," he said with a soft smile. "But if you hate it, I'll stop."

Truthfully? I didn't hate it as much as I pretended to. But I let the moment pass. Then he gave me a curious—but almost impressed—look.

"But seriously… how are you so good at basketball? I mean, no offense, but a girl like you seems like you'd be into cheerleading or acting—like one of those shiny, stuck-up girls."

"Um, no? I like basketball. I've always played. Sometimes I dream of going pro, like Kobe Bryant."

He mumbled under his breath, "You probably will. With skills like yours…"

I pretended not to hear him. "What was that?"

"Nothing," he said quickly, brushing it off like he hadn't said a word.

We walked in silence for a bit, talking about basketball and random stuff, until I finally changed the subject.

"Okay, this might sound weird, but… who's your date to the dance?"

He laughed and looked away. "Date? Uh… she's in our class."

"Our class?" I tilted my head.

"Yeah. She's got curly black hair in a bun. She's smart. Beautiful."

I thought for a moment—there weren't many girls in our class who fit that exact description.

Before I could guess, he added, "Oh, and she's Black."

There was only one Black girl in our class.

"Are you talking about me?" I asked slowly.

He met my eyes and smiled. "Yeah."

I stopped in my tracks. My jaw dropped. Caleb—of all people?

This was the same guy who used to call me names throughout the year. The same guy who dumped slime on my head days ago. The guy who never let a week go by without teasing me.

And now, he was asking me to the dance?

I didn't know what to say. Part of me wanted to say yes—I mean, he looked... cute when he smiled. And my best friends would finally stop bugging me about not having a date.

But then again, this was Caleb. *The* Caleb. What if it was just another prank? What if I said yes and looked stupid later? I wasn't even sure I'd be going to the party in the first place.

But somehow, what came out of my mouth was: "Yes—uh, why not?"

Don't ask me why I was even blushing.

His smile widened. "Really? I thought for sure you'd say no."

"Why?"

"Well, because we kind of don't like each other?"

"Then why ask me?"

"I don't know. I guess I just wanted to. Besides, it's just a dance— not a proposal. I figured it could be friendly."

"It is," I agreed. "But just so you know, we're not in a relationship now just because I said yes. Got it?"

"Of course, Hoopster—I mean, Jorelle."

CHAPTER 8

The next day passed quickly, then graduation day came. It was unforgettable. The auditorium buzzed with excitement, and the entire town seemed to hold its breath for us. Even the mayor made an appearance—his presence adding a strange weight to the moment, like what we were doing truly mattered.

When they called my name, I stepped onto the stage, nerves bubbling beneath my calm smile. I gave my speech—short, honest, maybe a little shaky—and accepted my certificate, hands trembling just slightly as reality set in.

I wasn't a little girl anymore. I wasn't just someone waiting to grow up. I had grown, at least a little. I was a teenager now, standing on the edge of everything I used to imagine.

Of course, it's not like everything changes overnight. I still have high school ahead of me, and university beyond that. There's so much left to become. But today wasn't for thinking ahead. Today was for living. For laughing. For dancing barefoot with my best friends under strings of fairy lights and paper streamers.

Today… we celebrate.

After the graduation, I saw Caleb talking to his friends, and I wanted to say hi. I told my mother and sister to wait for me in the car.

I approached Caleb and greeted him with a simple, "Hey."

He turned away from his friends and smiled, and we slipped behind the school building to talk privately.

"What's up?" he asked, leaning casually against the wall.

"So… how do you feel about graduating? Feels like we're stepping into adulthood," I said.

"Yeah, I suppose. Have you decided which high school you'll be attending?" he inquired.

"Not yet, but probably the one closest to home."

"Parkland High? That's a decent choice. So, are we still on for the dance tonight?"

"Absolutely," I replied.

"Good. See you there," he said, before returning to his group.

A subtle tension lingered between us—a quiet, unexpected connection. This wasn't our usual banter filled with teasing and insults; instead, there was an ease, a mutual smile exchanged, as if we were beginning something new.

Perhaps… I was developing feelings I hadn't anticipated.

CHAPTER 9

Back at home, Mom surprised me with a special gift. She went upstairs and returned carrying a large black bag, the words *Superior Bridal* printed boldly on it. *Bridal—like a bride,* I thought curiously.

"Jorelle, guess what I got!" Mama announced, handing me the bag.

"What is this?" I asked, eyeing the bag with a mix of confusion and curiosity.

"Just open it!" she urged eagerly.

Jirelle and Mama watched me expectantly as I unzipped the bag, revealing a stunning green floral dress. Delicate flowers adorned the waist and sides, and the fabric felt unbelievably smooth against my fingers.

"I got you a prom dress! Well, a dress for the dance tonight," Mama smiled.

"What? Oh my gosh, thank you, Mama! But you didn't have to," I exclaimed, both Jirelle and I shocked—though Jirelle's reaction was far less warm.

"Yeah, Mama, you really shouldn't have," she said sarcastically.

Mama frowned, turning to Jirelle. "What do you mean? Your sister needed a dress for the dance."

"Yeah, and you actually got her one? I can't believe it! You didn't even get me the outfit I always wanted," Jirelle snapped.

I thought she had moved past that.

But Mama answered firmly, "I'm sorry, but I work around the clock to provide for you both. It's not easy. And Jorelle's dress cost much less than yours—it'll be a while before I can afford yours. That's why I keep telling you to get a job, try to help me."

Jirelle fell silent, and I did too. Mama continued, her voice heavy with fatigue, "Ever since your father left—without money or support—I've struggled. I work through rain, snow, and sun so you both have food and shelter. Do you know how hard it was for me to get this apartment? The rent is $2,500 every month, and it's almost due."

A tear slipped down her cheek, and I realized how little I truly understood her sacrifices. If I had known, I wouldn't have insisted on the dress—though, truth be told, I didn't even know she had gotten it for me until now.

I glanced at Jirelle, silently urging her to speak.

She sighed and admitted, "Okay, I'm sorry. This time, I mean it. I didn't know. I just wanted that outfit so badly, and when you bought Jorelle's dress, I guess I got jealous."

Mama wiped her tears and assured Jirelle, "Don't worry, I'll get that for you."

"No, it's fine. You're right—I should get a job. And don't bother, I'll get my own outfit."

I stepped between them and pulled them into a hug. Looking at Mama, I said softly, "Mama, you don't have to do all this for us. We already appreciate you every day, especially after Dad left."

Then I turned to Jirelle and smiled. "And don't worry, sis—you can wear my dress anytime you want, as long as it fits."

CHAPTER 10

When it was time to go to the dance, I was a little bit late because I forgot to do my hair. It was so dry that I had to apply some moisturizer and add oil. My mom told me I didn't have much time, so I did a tucked-in chignon bun.

When I reached the school building, I met my best friends, and we all headed to the gym. While we were walking there, I looked at Tara and Erika and asked, "So, who're y'all's dates?"

Erika looked stunned and confused, but Tara uttered, "James."

"Huh?" I said, confused.

"The guy in our history class! He normally sits at the back, and he's so cute and tall—you know I like tall guys. Oh, and he said he's been having feelings for me for years!"

Erika and I looked at each other, stunned.

"So? What'd you do then?" Erika asked.

"So I gave him a chance—duh!" Tara said.

I was surprised. I didn't know Tara had a date. On a guy I barely even noticed in our history class?

Then I turned to Erika and asked, "And what about you?"

"Uh… I'm not into that date thing. I just decided to dance with my other friends who don't have dates—like me," Erika said.

"Oh, well, either we all have dates or not, we're still gonna have fun, right?" I said, opening the door to the gym.

"Yesss!" Tara exclaimed, walking in.

Erika and Tara then went to their dates—and friends—while I went to get a drink from the snack table. I was so thirsty, especially because I had to walk a mile to school since Mama's car was at the mechanic's, and I looked pale and dehydrated.

After I drank some cranberry juice and tried a few cake treats, I tried to spot Caleb in the crowd. Then Principal Wilkinson came on stage and said into the microphone, "Alright, our DJ is going to play some smooth, slow-mo songs for us to dance to!"

I was starting to get really worried that Caleb had ditched me— that he hadn't even come. I still couldn't find him, and everyone was already dancing with their dates and having fun.

But then I saw him. I saw him with... with a different girl. A random girl I'd never seen in our class—or even at our school. I was confused and headed straight toward them.

"What the heck is going on?" I demanded. They both froze, startled by my sudden appearance.

"Jorelle, you're here," Caleb said, clearly surprised to see me.

"Of course, I'm here! Did you really think I wouldn't come, just so you could dance with someone else?"

"Look, it's not what you think, I just—"

I crossed my arms with a fierce look and blurted out, "You just what? Thought dancing with some random girl would make me jealous? Well, it didn't! Maybe this is one of your stupid pranks!"

"No, it's not! This is Amanda—she's just a friend. Yeah, we're enemies, but I'd never pull a prank like that on you. I was even trying to stop—"

"No, you didn't. I can tell you didn't. You just broke my heart, Caleb. I thought we were past being enemies—maybe frenemies, at least. How could you lie to me and dance with another girl right in front of me?"

Amanda stepped in. "Well, you weren't here, and Caleb was waiting patiently, so I guess he had no choice but to dance with me."

I was furious.

Amanda pressed on, "And Caleb? He's a traitor. He's lied to every girl in school—just like he did to me on our date last year."

Caleb looked mortified. "Amanda! How could you?"

But she just walked away, joining her friends. I stared at Caleb, humiliated and disappointed. He looked back at me, stunned and embarrassed. Without another word, I fled the gym and headed to the parking lot, sinking onto a bench beneath a streetlight.

CHAPTER 11

After ten minutes, Caleb came to sit beside me, and I was just about ready to go back to the gym. But before I could even try to get up, he held my hand and said,

"Please, stay."

As much as I didn't want to look at his annoying face or talk to him, I still turned and asked, "Why did you do that?"

He sighed and said, "I—I actually don't know. I guess I got tired of thinking you wouldn't come. But… when you were late, I was so bored I danced with… my ex."

"She—she's your ex?"

"Yeah."

I never would have guessed that Caleb—the boy everyone in school seemed to dislike—actually had a girlfriend. Honestly, who would even want to be with him?

Still, I told him, "You do realize you broke my heart, right? My mom surprised me with this fifty–dollar dress, which I know she's been saving for something important. Honestly, I didn't even want to come tonight. I'm painfully introverted, but I didn't want to let you down."

He sighed. "I know. I'm sorry. Normally, I wouldn't apologize for betraying you—I'd laugh it off with my friends, say it was just a prank."

I interrupted, "Like that slime prank?"

He nodded. "Yeah. But Jorelle, the truth is… I like you. When I'm mean, it's usually because I have feelings I don't know how to handle."

I was stunned. Caleb—with all his arrogance and cruelty—actually liked me? And we were supposed to be enemies?

"You like me? Since when?" I asked, still trying to process it.

"Since I dumped that slime on your head. I felt terrible afterward and realized you didn't deserve it. And when you suddenly made that shot in basketball practice, my feelings got worse, I guess." I hesitated. "Do you really mean that?"

"Maybe I do, maybe I don't. But I have feelings for you—and it's okay if you don't feel the same."

The truth was, I did like him. Ever since kindergarten, when people used to *ship* us, I'd secretly had a crush. Even after he became cruel and played pranks, I never stopped liking him—I just kept it hidden.

So I smiled and said, "No, I actually do like you."

He raised an eyebrow, surprised. "Really?"

"Yes. But does that mean you'll finally stop the pranks and teasing?"

"Of course."

I brushed his cheek with a soft kiss and smiled. He blushed and returned the gesture with a kiss on my lips. I think I blushed even harder.

Then he said, "By the way, you look stunning in that dress."

I smiled warmly. "Thank you. You don't look too bad yourself."

"Thanks. Now, shall we head back to the dance and start fresh?"

"Absolutely," I replied, rising to my feet.

We returned to the gym, moving together to the slow, smooth music. As we danced, I suddenly realized we were right in the center of the room, like we were under a spotlight—and I loved every second of being there with him.

The DJ switched the track to a high–energy hip–hop beat, and the crowd erupted, dancing wildly. Caleb and I fell into the rhythm of a favorite dance we'd invented back in fifth grade, laughing and moving as if no one else was around. Every moment was pure joy—a memory I knew I'd carry with me forever.

THE COST OF BELONGING

"Sometimes fitting in costs more than it's worth."

CHAPTER 1

Gigi was the name everyone called me, but my birth name is actually Georgia. I guess Gigi was cuter and better, and I've never argued about that.

I'm starting a new school today because I just moved to Seattle, in America, and had to change schools. My dad got a new job here, so we just had to move away. Anyway, I'm not that upset because I have my best friend, Alexa. She somehow convinced her parents to let her move in with me—but only for three months. Still, I'm glad she decided to come. I mean, I have no siblings, and my friends are… well, I don't know, but they're just not useful in my life, ya know?

Anyway, today at breakfast, Alexa and I wanted to get school supplies for our new school, but my parents wanted us to go out as a family instead. And I really wanted to buy stuff for school because we only had two days left.

I got out of my chair and said to my parents, "Mom, Dad, please! This is my only chance to get all the things I need for school if I have to fit in."

"But honey, you know we're going for a family day," Mom said.

"But that's not fair! I mean, this 'family day' thing you made up is so not cool."

"Gigi! This is the time to spend with your family, and you're not going to buy anything for school because you already have what you need," Mom scolded me.

I stormed off to my room with an angry face.

Later on, Alexa came in and saw me on the computer.

She asked, "Uh, Gigi, what're you doing?"

"I'm trying to find good shops to go to," I said, busy typing on the computer.

"Why?" She came closer to see.

"Because we need to get those things for school, ya know?"

"But your mom said no."

"So? Look, if she really wants to make me happy at our new school, then she should agree to let us get those things. And besides, she'll never know, because I won't tell her—nor would you, right?"

"Uh, yeah, totally," she muttered under her breath.

"Good. Now, let me try to find one shop… aha! I found one."

"Really? What's it called?"

"School Supply Store—and it's ten minutes from here."

"Oh, so we can walk there."

"Yeah! C'mon, we're going now." I got up, already wearing my shoes.

"Wait, we're sneaking out?" she paused.

"Well, it's not really sneaking out—it's like… uh, look, we're fourteen now, it doesn't really matter."

"What about your mom?"

"Alexa, what did I just say? She won't find out, because we won't tell her. Now c'mon!"

I dragged her out.

CHAPTER 2

When we arrived, we picked up lead pencils—not the regular kind, but the glowing ones. We also grabbed large erasers, the artistic type, and a set of tall, slender bottles. I mean, Alexa took the skinny long ones, and I took a Stanley Cup. And my gosh, it cost a lot.

"Gigi! That's $40! We don't have that much money for that!"

"Oh, Alexa, I wonder—how are you still my best friend? I mean, seriously, you never agree to anything! Like I said, it's fine."

"Alright, fine." She rolled her eyes.

"Great! Let's go pay."

When we got to the cashier, the whole pack of stuff we bought was $59.99! That was way over our budget.

"Whoa! This is way too much. Way more than I expected," I said, staring right at the price.

"I told you," Alexa said, shrugging.

I gulped. While we were walking back home, Alexa kept on looking at me like I had done something bad.

"What?" I asked, turning to her.

"We just bought expensive stuff!" She raised her hands dramatically in the air.

"So? No big deal."

"No big deal? Gigi, all these things cost $60. It *is* a big deal!"

"Relax, at least we had the money to pay for it."

"Yeah, we had $100—now we have $40! What are you going to do with $40? Buy toy plushies?"

"Oh, c'mon. I know you're happy you bought that stuff. Look, I'm also surprised. But let's not make it too obvious. You know how my parents are gonna react—especially my mom."

"Ugh!" She quickened her pace and reached the house before I did.

The next morning came by quickly, but I woke up to yelling in my ears. I got dressed and went downstairs to see Mom shouting and Dad trying to calm her down.

"What's going on?" I asked, still tired.

"Gigi Elizabeth Blythe!" Oh boy, what did I do now?

"Uh, yes?" I asked, already getting scared.

"You went out last night to get stuff I told you not to get? Hm? And you dared to spend $60 on stupid things you really don't need!"

"What? Ho–how did you find out?"

"That doesn't matter right now! All I need you to do is tell me *why* and *how* you dared to go out last night."

"You know why."

Then I went back to my room and slammed the door without saying a word. I didn't have the time to explain—I was already tired. I woke up Alexa, and I immediately thought of something.

"You told them!" I frowned angrily.

"What are you talking about?" she mumbled, scratching her eyes.

"You told them about last night! How could you? I trusted you!"

"I—I don't know, okay?! I just... I knew—we knew—it was a bad idea, and you know I don't do bad stuff like that, so I told them. I'm sorry."

"Alexa, what's bad about us earning money and using it to buy stuff we know we need for school?"

"Uh—one, disrespecting your parents. Two, buying stuff—yes, we do need it—but it's useless because all the things your mom bought are the same thing. It's just a simple, common shape and color! Also, she told us not to!"

I went quiet for a while and just lay on my bed. I wanted to cry, but as a 14-year-old, I couldn't do that—and I didn't want my own best friend (who betrayed me) to see me upset about such things. So I tried to hold it back.

"Gigi, seriously, I'm sorry. I really am. Please, we can talk about it, not ignore each other," Alexa pleaded.

"Just... leave me alone for now."

"Alright."

I was still really angry about what she did. I mean, I trusted her. And I didn't even think she would do that. Now my mom is probably going to ground me for two whole weekends with no going out—apart from *family day*.

CHAPTER 3

At dinner, my mom told me something I definitely didn't want to agree with.

"Gigi, I'm going to have to take the stuff you bought."

"What? Why?" I dropped my fork on my plate.

"Because you don't need it. I've told you several times."

"No. I'm not taking it away."

"You're not the one taking it away—I am. It's not your choice."

"But it's my stuff, and I bought it with my own money! It's not fair that you get to take it away like that."

"Gigi, I'm not asking you, I'm telling you. You could have thought about not buying it, and you wouldn't be in that much trouble."

"Ugh!"

I got out of my chair and went back upstairs. I went to bed and started crying again. I didn't want my summer or school year to be like this. All I wanted was to buy my own stuff for school, hang out with my best friend, and have a good time with my family in this new city.

Not this—having my mom buy my school stuff (which is not cool and so common), my best friend betraying me, and a horrible day with my family.

Anyway, later in the day, as I was writing in my diary, Mom knocked on the door and asked,

"Can I come in?"

"Yeah," I answered in a dull voice.

She sat on Alexa's bed and said, "Look, I know you're pretty sad, but… you know those things aren't really useful right now. And going out alone at night is way too dangerous."

"But I went with Alexa, and I'm 14 years old. There's no need to worry about me."

"And I'm your mom—it's my job to worry about you. It's called parenting."

"Well, you don't need to parent me because, luckily, nothing happened. And I don't know how you don't care about me walking alone to school, but you're worried about me going out."

"You don't walk alone to school—you go with Alexa. And you went out yesterday to the shop. *At night.* That's more dangerous than going out during the day."

"So? Like I said, I'm 14 now. I don't need my parents' supervision. I'm fine—alone or not."

"Your dad and I decided you won't be going out in the day or night for a month. And even if you try to sneak out, we'll eventually find out and make it two months."

"What?! C'mon! You've already taken away my stuff that, yes, I *really* do need for school—and now you're making me stay home for a month? No way!"

"Yes, way! You made us really angry last night and even dragged your best friend into it. Of course, we'll punish you!"

"But—"

"No more complaints! Just get ready for family day. We'll be going to a restaurant first."

"Ugh! This is so unfair!"

I went straight to the bathroom and sank to the floor, crying. I didn't want to be anywhere else. I just wanted a good school year with my best friend. But how could I, when she'd snitched and betrayed me?

And now, I was grounded for a whole month.

"My life is so miserable."

CHAPTER 4

After I cried for about five minutes, I heard a knock on the bathroom door.

"What?" I asked, still irritated.

"Uh… your mom wanted to make sure you're done." It was Alexa.

"Are we going now?" I wiped the dried tears off my face.

"Yeah, so you have to hurry up."

"Okay, I'll be ready."

I immediately changed into my outfit and left the bathroom. In the car, Mom looked at me like she was worried about something and asked,

"Honey, you know, we can go to your favorite restaurant."

"Why?" I asked, acting like I didn't care.

"Well, I know you're pretty angry right now, so…"

"I don't care."

"Huh?" She glanced at the car mirror, tilting it toward me.

"Whatever restaurant is fine!"

Dad sprang right into action and yelled,

"Hey! Don't shout at your mom like that!"

"Whatever," I muttered, annoyed.

After that horrendous family day, I went to bed, closed my eyes, and dreamt of tomorrow—being at school, having good friends, and having a good day.

Alexa then came into the room, wrapped in a towel, her hair still damp.

"Are you okay?" she asked while drying her hair with the towel.

"Yeah, why wouldn't I be?" I opened my eyes.

"Um, well… because today, you weren't exactly thrilled."

"Oh, why would I *be* happy today?"

"Okay, Gigi, I know you're really angry about that night, but… I—I really am sorry. And if I hadn't told your parents, they would've found out eventually and probably told my mom about it. And I wouldn't be here anymore."

I sat up on my bed and asked, confused, "What do you mean you wouldn't be here?"

"I'd be on a plane back to Las Vegas."

"Why?"

"Because I made a promise. I promised my mom that I'd be on my best behavior—including being honest and respectful. And she trusted me. Even if I did something bad, your parents would tell my mom, and I'd be in trouble when I go back home."

She then looked down in misery.

"So… there was no choice but to tell my parents."

"Oh."

I was really surprised—because if we had kept the secret, my best friend would've been leaving me here, in this city and new school, and going back to Las Vegas. All because of me.

She came to sit beside me on the bed and held my hand.

"Look, I know we were supposed to keep it a secret, but those things were exactly the stuff your mom bought for us. But these are just… I don't know, regular and old-fashioned. But it doesn't matter— it doesn't matter how we dress to school or what things we bring. Because even if kids bully us for it, I know I've got my best friend beside me to beat them up!"

We both giggled.

"Gigi, you're my best friend—my *only* best friend. The first person who became my friend. You're always by my side. So let's not let school stuff get into our heads. It's gonna be our first day of school, and… I want it to be the best first day of school, okay?"

I smiled and hugged her.

"Okay."

"And I'm sorry for getting angry at you. I was just… so happy, and then that happened."

"It's okay. But I hope you can forgive me."

"Totally."

CHAPTER 5

"Wake up, bestie! It's the first day of school!"

I opened my eyes, yawning the whole time, and asked, "What time is it?"

"It's... 7:15," Alexa said, checking her phone.

"Oh, Alexa, 7:15? C'mon, we have more time! Please, let me sleep for about... five minutes," I said, going back to sleep.

Then, after five—sorry, twenty—minutes, Alexa came back into the room and started hitting me to wake me up.

"Ughh, Alexa!" I said, annoyed.

"Wake up! It's already twenty minutes past, and your mom told me to come wake you up."

"So? Another... five minutes," I groaned.

She sighed dramatically, then suddenly shrieked, "Oh my gosh! Gigi, there are roaches on the floor!"

I immediately jumped up and yelled, "Where?!"

Alexa started laughing like a maniac.

"What? Roaches aren't funny!" I looked around for them.

"Nothing—it's just... there are no roaches! Haha!"

I grabbed one of my pillows and threw it at her.

"Seriously?"

"It was the only way to wake you up. Now let's go! It's 7:30 now." She slipped on her shoes.

"What?!"

We reached school. I took a deep breath.

"It's gonna be fine," I told myself. Even though I couldn't do my own school shopping with my best friend, nothing's going to happen.

We entered the school—and my gosh, it was big. Bigger than my old school back in Las Vegas.

We saw a lady who looked like a guidance counselor, so we went up to her and asked,

"Hi, are you the guidance counselor?"

"Yes! Need any help?" She clasped her hands together.

"Yeah, we're new here and need to get to our first class."

"Oh, okay. Can I get your names first?"

"I'm Blythe Gigi, and she's Beali Alexa."

"Okay, well, unfortunately, you'll be in different classes."

Alexa raised her eyebrows. "Like… separated?"

"Yes. So, Alexa, your class is in room 213—down the hall to your left. And Gigi, your class is in room 204, just two doors down the hall."

"Uh, okay. Thanks."

Oh no! We're going to be separated? No way! I can't live a day without Alexa. She's like a twin sister to me—and now we're going to be in different classes? Who am I going to talk to? Or partner with, in case?

"I'm so sorry, bestie, but… like I said, you got this! *We* got this," Alexa said, smiling.

"But what if I have my panic attack again?!" I said nervously.

"Don't worry, it's gonna be fine. It's just the first day. Once we get used to it, we won't even be worrying about it."

"Alright. But! Just in case of anything, come to the bathroom in ten minutes. You know I always want to check how you and the classes are."

"Okay." She nodded.

Then we separated and went to our classes.

I took a deep breath again. In my class, we had Algebra, and since I was new here, the teacher wanted me to introduce myself to the class. No way! I hated that, especially when it had to be in public. It always made me feel like I was about to have a panic attack. But I tried—and I did it. I said hello, my name, age, and favorite subject.

"Well, thank you, Gigi. You can sit between those two girls in the middle," the teacher said.

When I sat down, the girls started whispering to me.

"I like your name—it's giving… famous influencer," the brunette-looking Latina girl said.

"And I like your outfit," the blonde girl added.

"Um, thanks. What are your names?" I asked.

"I'm Angelina, but I prefer Ange," the brunette said.

"And I'm Faye," the blonde added.

"Nice names," I nodded.

CHAPTER 6

After that class, I waited for Alexa to come out of hers. And while I was waiting, the same two girls came up to me and asked, "Hey! Wanna go to lunch with us?"

I wanted to, but… I had to wait for my best friend. Still, I was making friends, so… I was sure she could look for me in the cafeteria.

I answered, "Sure."

In the cafeteria, I sat at a table with other people from different classes. I guessed Ange and Faye already knew them since they were all talking, and I was just there, staring at them.

Then Ange looked at me and said, "Oh! Guys, this is Gigi. Gigi, these are my other friends. Only two of them are in our class."

I said hi—and that's when I saw Alexa coming to the table. She sat beside me and gave me a look. An angry look.

I asked, "What's wrong?"

"Are you seriously asking me that? You didn't wait for me after class, and you didn't text me where you'd be going!"

"Uh, the cafeteria? Where else? And also, I've made friends, so I couldn't wait for you."

"Just because you made friends doesn't mean you can't wait for your own best friend! And you never went to the bathroom anyway!"

"Wait—you did? Ha! I didn't actually think you would. It was supposed to be a joke."

"Well, it's not funny! I thought you weren't ready for school."

"Well… like you said, it's gonna be fine—and it was."

Faye saw us talking and asked, "Who's that?"

"Uh, this is my friend," I said, turning to Faye.

"Really? 'Friend'?" Alexa said, then walked out.

What did I even do?

When school ended, I tried calling Dad to come pick us up, but he wasn't available—he was out shopping. So I called Mom and waited for her.

While we were waiting, I saw Alexa sitting on the school stairs outside, frowning.

I sat next to her and asked, "What's wrong now?"

She muttered, "Nothing."

"I know something's wrong. C'mon, tell me."

"You." She swallowed hard.

"Huh?"

"You're the problem."

"Wha—what did I do?" I leaned back a bit.

Alexa slowly looked up at me with a spiteful face. "Friend? Am I actually your friend?"

"Uh, yeah? Aren't you?"

"We're best friends, Gigi! Not friends."

"Oh, is this about—look, I'm so sorry about that. I didn't mean it."

"First, you make me go to the bathroom alone every ten minutes, then you don't tell me that you're going to the cafeteria, and then I see you sitting with some bunch of... random girls from your class!"

"They're my friends! And you can be too."

"How? Gigi, I only came to be with you—to go to a new school with you. And now, on our first day, you're already having friends?"

"Isn't that... what you said we should focus on?"

"Ugh!" She got up, more furious.

CHAPTER 7

Before I could speak, I heard a car honk—and that's when I realized it was my mom.

In the car, Mom saw our depressed faces and asked, "Uh, so... how was school?"

We didn't answer at first. Then Mom asked again, and I replied, "Good! It was good."

"Okay, well then, tell me what happened."

Alexa raised her head and uttered, "Okay, so—" But before she could continue, I looked at her with a *please don't tell her* face. Still, she went on.

"So, we had a good day, like Gigi said. But... our math teacher was really strict, and we weren't in the same class." She smiled at me, and I smiled back.

"Aw, sorry, girls. The school actually told me you wouldn't be in the same class for the year... but at least you still have each other."

The next morning was the same—we ate, and Mom talked about another family time.

But at school, it was different.

In English class, Ange and Faye kept talking to me about going to the new mall near the school. I'd never seen or even heard of a new mall, so I asked, "What new mall?"

Ange leaned back in her chair and said, "Milliken Mall. It just opened last week."

Faye added, "And thousands of people are going there—mostly because all the shops are high-end brands!"

"What do you mean?"

"It's like, you know… Louis Vuitton, Gucci, and stuff," Faye answered.

"And we're planning on going there today," Ange uttered.

"Oh, cool! Hope you guys have fun," I said, turning back to the board.

"Uh, we're thinking of going… on lunch break, though," she added.

"But that's illegal. You can't go anywhere while on school premises."

"Yeah, but we can't even go after school because our moms won't allow us. And some boys will be going there during lunch break anyway, so we thought of going with them," Faye said, winking jokingly.

"But—"

Ange interrupted me. "C'mon! It'll be fun. And besides, no one will know because… we'll be going during lunch break. Technically sneaking out."

"Yeah, don't you want new branded stuff?" Faye added.

I sighed. "Alright, but can I come?"

"Of course you can!" Ange said.

Now, there was a problem. I didn't want to leave my best friend alone at school. She was newer than me, and she didn't have any friends yet. Plus, I had just made her angry yesterday. I didn't want her to get mad again because I left her without telling her. Even though I still wanted to go out to this mall of theirs, and check it out.

At lunch break, the girls told me they had to use the washroom and said I should wait for them. While I was waiting, I saw someone running toward me. I turned—and it was Alexa.

"Where have you been? I've been looking for you everywhere!"
"Uh… I just used the bathroom. I guess the lunch I ate yesterday wanted to come out." I rubbed my neck nervously.

"Oh, really? Look, Gigi, I know you're hiding something and you're not telling me."

"That's not true… uh—how about you go to the cafeteria first, and then I'll come?"

"Why not come now?"

"Uh, because I just forgot something in class. Be right back!"

Then I hurried to the classroom, hoping she would wait for me in the cafeteria.

CHAPTER 8

After waiting for Ange and Faye to finish, we finally went to the mall. And my gosh, it was… huge. And so… creative. The roof was made of glass, and it looked like broken, shattered glass. All the shop windows were also made of glass, but they were so tinted you couldn't even catch a glimpse of your reflection.

We went to three different shops and spent about twenty minutes there. We met some of the boys from school and hung out with them. But then there was another problem.

We decided to go to one last shop before heading home, but right before we chose which one, we heard a loud voice coming from behind us. When I turned, I saw a policeman coming our way. Ange and Faye immediately started to run, but then I heard someone yell, "Don't you dare run away!"

Everybody in the mall turned to look at us—and it was *so* embarrassing. Then I saw two ladies walking toward us, and I instantly knew it was Mom and Alexa.

The police took all the things we'd bought and returned them to the shops.

Ange started resisting and yelling, "But we bought those!"

The policeman ignored her and asked my mom if she wanted to press charges for leaving school grounds and shoplifting.

But the thing is—we didn't shoplift. Yes, we left school without permission, but we *bought* everything with our own money.

My mom looked at us for a while and said, "Uh, no, I don't want any charges."

The policeman nodded and said everything was settled. But we wouldn't be going to school for three days—because we were suspended.

In the car, I could feel Mom was very angry, even though she didn't show it. I was really mad at Alexa, though, because she got the police involved in this. All she could have done was tell the principal, and then the principal would've called my parents, found me, and taken me home.

I looked at Mom and said, "Mom, I'm really sorry. I didn't know what I was thinking."

"Gigi, this is the second time you're doing this! Why?"

"I… I don't know! I'm just sorry."

"Sorry, can't fix anything, and you can't make this up."

I started crying. Mom was right—I couldn't make anything up for this.

She kept going. "And I can't believe you dragged your best friend into this. She had to watch you almost get arrested. Is this how you treat your friends, huh?"

Then she turned to Alexa and started apologizing for what she had dealt with. I couldn't even speak. I was setting such a bad example for my family.

"By next week, you'll be in a new school," Mom said firmly. "I'm not going to watch my own child sneak into malls and shoplift."

I wanted to tell her we didn't actually shoplift—but... that would've only made things worse.

CHAPTER 9

The next morning, Mom knocked on my door and came in. She woke us up and told us to start packing our stuff. I asked why, and she said,

"Because we'll be going to a new home in the next two days. Apparently, the new school you'll be attending is in a different place."

Alexa and I were really shocked. We didn't even stay in that school for a week!

Speaking of school, I heard on social media that Ange and Faye's moms actually filed charges—and made them go to jail! I was so glad my mom didn't arrest or charge me. Then I realized something.

I immediately rushed downstairs to where Mom was, sat beside her, and hugged her.

"What's going on?" she asked, confused.

"Just hugging my mom."

"Are you trying to make up for what you did last night? Because I'll tell you—it's not going to work."

"Oh, c'mon, Mom. Look, I'm just glad you didn't get me arrested."

"Really?"

"Yeah. I just heard my friends who were with me at the mall got arrested."

"But I didn't charge them."

"Well… their moms did."

"Oh. Well, I'm your mother, and I care for you. Even though sometimes you can be so stubborn, I still love you." She kissed my forehead.

"I love you too." I was glad my mom could forgive me now.

I continued, "So… is everything okay now?"

"Uh, no. You still have another person waiting for an apology."

I thought it was Dad or maybe the principal—but then I realized it was Alexa.

CHAPTER 10

I went upstairs and saw her packing her stuff into a suitcase. I walked closer and said, "Um, can we talk?"

She turned to me, looking annoyed, and said, "What?"

"Look, I know I've been a little weird and annoying and stuff, but... I want to make it up to you."

"And how do you plan to do that?"

"By saying sorry. You deserve an apology. I was stupid enough to lie to you and leave you at school alone."

"Yeah, with some weird girls."

"Oh, they're definitely weird!"

Alexa let out a small laugh, then said, "Gigi, like I said, you're my best friend. And everything's gonna be okay—but it won't happen if we go our separate ways. Remember what we promised?"

"Uh... remind me again?" I chuckled, a little confused.

"That we'll always be with each other—and go everywhere together."

"Yes. And Alexa, I don't want you to be just a friend to me, because you're everything—my bestie, partner in crime, sister, and buddy."

"Forever?"

"Forever."

We hugged.

And that was the last time we'd ever fight—or leave each other—again.

SICK DAHLIA

"Illness doesn't always equal death."

CHAPTER 1

They say *Dahlia* means *flower*—something soft, delicate, always needing care. Maybe that's what I've always been. Born with Fabry disease, my body has never had the strength to run, climb, or chase the wind like other kids. The doctors said my cells couldn't break down fat properly—that it would stay with me forever. So I've been homeschooled, tucked away in quiet rooms while the world moved on outside.

But this week, everything changes. My disease decided to give me a chance, so I'm going to school. Since I'm about to be a teen, I have to start school.

But today, I'll be going to the hospital for an appointment. As I was going downstairs, my mom stopped me and asked, "Wait, did you take your extra medication for the disease?"

I answered with a sigh, "Yes, ma'am."

"Okay, and did you also take your anti-seizure drugs for pains?"

"Yes. Now, can we go?"

My mom has always been worried about me. Not that I hate it—it's just... I'm responsible for my health now, and it's not a big deal anymore. Not even Dad or my little sister acts like that.

CHAPTER 2

When we got to the hospital, the doctor, Mr. Donnach, checked my blood veins, did some pharynx tests, and told us some good news.

"So, I've realized Dahlia's enzymes are reacting well to our surgery from last time. I guess you've been taking your medication and your ERTs, Dahlia?"

"Uh, yes," I uttered.

"Um, so… does it mean we won't be having many appointments, doctor?" Mom asked.

"Yes, I think so. I mean, I can tell how great Dahlia's health is, so appointments should be reduced now."

"Oh, good!" Mom said happily.

"But there is one issue," Dr. Donnach added.

"What issue?" Dad asked.

"We've been doing tests on her enzymes, and it seems she's been having mitral valve prolapses."

"What's that?" Mom asked, getting worried.

"It means one of the heart's doors doesn't close properly and kind of pushes the wrong way when the heart beats," Dr. Donnach answered.

"Oh, but how is that happening?" Dad asked.

"Well, it may be a symptom of Dahlia's blood vessels getting weak."

"Wait—so if I'm getting weaker and continuously heating up, doesn't that mean I'll also be fainting due to loss of strength?!" I asked, scared.

"Well, not really. But it's possible—"

"Then how can she focus on schoolwork? She's going to be worried about it all the time!" Mom said.

"We can still help her manage her symptoms, though." Dr. Donnach said.

"Are you kidding me? Mom, how can I pass in school now? I'll probably be the dumbest kid there!" I got up and shouted.

"Honey, it's okay, everything will be fine," Mom said, trying to calm me down.

But I still couldn't believe this. I was so happy that my health was getting better, and I was finally about to go to school. And now this? What could get worse?

CHAPTER 3

The next morning, I ate breakfast with a frown on my face. I wasn't having a good day, and I knew it wouldn't get any better. My parents asked if I wanted to continue my school shopping spree, but I didn't feel like it. Ever since I heard about my enzyme problem, I haven't felt like myself.

My little sister, Olivia, came downstairs, jumping up and down like a puppy or something, and smiling.

"What's with the happy attitude?" Mom asked.

"Oh, I didn't have time to tell you yesterday since you were out with Dahlia, so I decided to tell you today!" Olivia said, sitting down.

"What?" Dad asked.

"I got a ticket to Wonderland!!" she replied.

"Oh, really?" Mom asked, not even shocked.

"Yep! And I'm so excited—I finally get to go to a place I've always wanted to go!"

Olivia had always been begging to go to Wonderland. But my parents never agreed because we live so far from where Wonderland is, and they're always busy trying to get my health better. She even tried to bribe people for ticket money, but of course, no one fell for it.

"Can I please go this time?" Olivia asked, giving Mom and Dad puppy eyes.

"Are you sure it's not another bribe you pulled on poor, innocent people to get money for a ticket?" I asked, curious.

She answered with an annoyed face, "Uh, no? I promise it's a real ticket."

"But honey, you know we won't have time to take you to Wonderland. It's way too far, and we have to deal with another problem from your sister," Mom said.

"Another? Why is it always Dahlia? When is it my time for you guys to care about me?!" Olivia shouted, then stormed off upstairs.

I felt really bad. I mean, she was right—it's always been me that Mom and Dad cared about the most. Not even care... worry. And she finally did something good to get that ticket, but again, they said no.

CHAPTER 4

While I was in my room, I heard a knock, and it was Olivia. I told her to come in, and when she did, she was crying. I stopped what I was doing and told her to tell me what was wrong.

"Why are Mom and Dad always concerned about you and not me?" she mumbled.

I sighed and said, "Olivia, you know it's not that. They do have concern for you—it's just... my health condition is very serious and has to be taken care of most of the time. And you know how much they worry when it comes to something like this."

"But they're always asking about you, stressing about you, and definitely care about you more. I'm like a ghost here—I'm invisible to them."

"No, you're not. They care about you, I know that."

"Are you sure?"

"I promise my red little heart that they care about you. But do you know I actually hate it when they worry about me more than you?" I furrowed my eyebrows.

"Really?" she chuckled.

"Yeah! I mean, you're the youngest here—you should be the one getting more attention." I smiled.

"But you're sick. You need way more attention!" she snickered.

"Exactly! Now you get it. Now, c'mon—wanna go school shopping with me?"

"Yes!"

Later that day, my family and I went to the shopping centre down the street. For once, I wasn't weighed down by thoughts of my condition. All I could think about was Olivia and me, laughing together—and my parents, not worrying, not hovering, but simply enjoying the moment with us. Maybe my day had turned out better after all.

CHAPTER 5

Today, I was finally going to school—middle school, actually. I got up, got ready, and went downstairs with a happy face.

"Oh, somebody is excited about something in her life," Mom said, dishing my breakfast.

I answered with a smile, "Yeah, I mean, I've been homeschooled my whole life, and it's finally time for me to see how the real world is in school."

"But aren't you worried about the doctor's news?" Dad asked, a little off-topic.

Mom hit him on the shoulder and said, "You didn't have to bring that up!"

"It's okay, Mom. But I think I've got it managed now, Dad. Like, I think I can do this—I *know* I can do this!" I said boldly.

"That's my girl!" Dad smiled and winked at me.

"Okay then," Mom said, "if you're ready, then let's go," and grabbed her keys.

I reached school, kissed my mom on the cheek, and said goodbye.

When I entered, it was so big, and a lot of people were walking and talking to each other. It felt like I was invisible, though nobody knew I was the new girl. On my class map schedule, it said I had Science for the first period, so I tried to find the Science class—but that's when the bell rang, and everyone started to run to their classes.

And there I was, alone, standing in the middle of the hall, confused about where to go. I started to panic—and when I panic, my body heats up so fast, and my vision was blurred. I started hallucinating. I didn't know what to do at all. But that's when I heard a voice saying, "Dahlia! Over here!"

I turned to see who it was, and it was a teacher standing at a classroom door, waving at me. I went to her and asked, "Uh, is this the Science class? That's my first period."

She smiled and said, "Yes! Come on in."

I went in and saw all the kids staring at me, whispering to each other, and giving looks. I didn't know if they were talking about me, but it was giving me bad vibes. I sat beside a short, dark-haired girl, and it seemed like she knew me.

I mumbled, "Uh, hi… I'm Dahlia."
She smiled and said, "I know. Everybody knows you."
"Really?" I raised my eyebrows.
"Yep. The principal came to the class yesterday and told us you were coming. She said you even have an… enzyme problem, right?"

Wait—if she knows, the class knows, and the teacher knows, that means my parents told them. They told them about my health problem! Great, now everyone knows about my Fabry disease.

"Uh, yes, I do have a health problem," I answered with a little frown.

"I'm Mara, by the way. Nice to meet you!" She extended her hand, and I shook it.

CHAPTER 6

After the first class, we had lunch. I went to the cafeteria with Mara, and she introduced me to her other friends, Emily and Lizzie. I sat down and took out my lunch. When I started eating, they were all staring at me—like I was doing something weird.

One of the girls, Emily, asked the weirdest question, and I was so confused.

"Um, what are you eating?" she said.

Lizzie then asked, "Is that… a hot dog but with gravy and a sandwich?"

Okay, first, it's not *'gravy and a sandwich.'* It's bread with gravy in it because I have to eat it enough so my body doesn't overheat. Especially when I have P.E., I have to make sure my levels are average—not high, not low—or else I'll faint.

So I answered, "Uh, no? It's just bread. The hot dog is just a snack."

"Oh, sorry. I thought it was diet food. Looked kind of weird."

That was absolutely rude. Just because I'm sick doesn't mean I eat weird food.

CHAPTER 7

At home, while we were having dinner, I told my family everything that happened at school—I told them about the lunch incident, and they thought it was unbelievable.

"Oh my Gosh, they actually said that?" Mom asked, surprised.

"Yeah! Can you believe that?" I said.

"At least they cared," Dad shrugged.

"What do you mean?" I asked.

"Well, they asked about your health problem, right?"

"Yeah, but I didn't want them to talk about it."

"Don't you want people to care about your health problem? Don't you want people to be friends with you? Then they have to know everything about you," Dad said.

"Dad, first—no, I don't want people to care *too much* about my health problem. You guys are already doing so much. And second, yes, I want friends, but not friends who have to know everything about me—like my personal information."

"Well, how do you expect them to know you more, then? How do you expect them to like you? Don't you want to fit in?" Dad asked.

"Yes, I want to fit in, but... you guys told everyone about my health problem! I didn't want them to know for a reason—but now everyone knows everything about me, because of you guys!"

"Honey—" Mom said.

I cut her off and went to my room, annoyed.

CHAPTER 8

The next day at school, there was an announcement that the whole school was going on a two-day trip to the woods. It was the first time I was ever going on a nature trip. In my whole life, the only trips I'd ever had were… doctor's appointments, Grandma's house visits, and New York—and that was just for my Fabry disease surgery.

Mara, who was sitting beside me, was really happy, though.

"Going on a two-day trip to the woods? That'll be so fun! I can't wait!" she said.

"How are you so happy? It's just a trip. And besides, what's so fun about the woods?" I asked.

"Uh, a lot! One: the woods are technically in the forest, so we're actually going to a forest—and I've *always* wanted to go to the woods because I love animals and nature! Two: it's a two-day trip—*two days!* Finally, no more school and no learning for two days!"

"Wow, I guess you really like the woods. Well, I don't really think I'll like going."

"Why?"

"In my whole life of going out, I've only gone to New York and doctor's appointments. It's not much. Also, I don't think going to the woods is a good idea. I mean, isn't it full of wild animals?"

"Well, Dahlia, I guess your life as a sick person isn't really great—but that's gonna change, because I promise it's gonna be so fun!"

"I guess. But know, being sick doesn't mean I can't have some fun, okay?"

"Okay, okay, whatever. C'mon, let's go get a permission form!"

At home, I gave the permission slip to my parents to sign, and they weren't exactly pleased to see it.

"What?" I asked, hoping they'd sign it.

"Honey, you're going to the woods?" Mom said, still shocked.

"Yeah, so?"

"Isn't it too dangerous? I mean, it's probably one of those woods with wild animals in it."

"I know, Mom, but it's fine. I'm gonna be fine. And besides, I won't be alone—almost the whole school is going. And if this is about the enzyme problem, you shouldn't be worried about it, because I—"

She interrupted me and said, "Okay, I get it! Just... promise me you're going to come back home safe and with no injuries?"

"Ugh, fine. Just sign it already!"

She and Dad signed the slip, and at last, I could finally have an experience worth calling my own.

CHAPTER 9

Today was the day we were going to the woods, and I ran into the crowd to find Mara. When I found her, she was talking to her other friends.

I went closer to them and said, "Hey, guys."

They turned to me and smiled.

"Hi. Are you actually ready for this?" Emily asked. She said it like I wasn't—and never was—ready for this.

"Yeah! Why ask?" I answered, confused. I mean, wasn't it obvious?

"Oh, nothing. I just thought your health problem was gonna affect your—"

Lizzie elbowed Emily's rib and whispered, "Shut up! That's rude."

"Look, guys, just because I'm sick doesn't mean I won't have fun on this trip. I'll be fine, so don't worry like my parents do, okay?" I declared.

We had only known each other for a day, and already my health was turning into their favorite topic. It wasn't like I was about to faint in the middle of a trip, yet they spoke as if it were that serious. Why did every fun moment have to circle back to me being sick? It was annoying—and honestly, a little rude.

"Yeah! You heard her, guys," Mara protested.

"You too, Mara," I chuckled.

On the bus, we were singing, dancing, and shouting happily. This was going to be the best trip ever.

When we arrived, there were cabins everywhere and a campfire. It was warm and quiet (apart from the school kids), and it was so green—the trees were green, the grass was dark green, and we could hear birds singing and chirping in the sky.

"Oh my gosh, this is so cool!" Mara said.

"Yeah, but there's much more, right?" I asked.

"Oh yeah! Just wait."

After waiting and waiting, we finally went for a walk around the forest.

"Please, everyone, don't get lost or touch anything that looks weird or toxic!" the principal yelled.

Well, as for me, I was going anywhere I wanted—so I might get lost. I ran around, seeing rivers and green swamps with colorful, moist frogs in them. The air around was smooth and perfect. The trees seemed alive with energy, breathing out into the warm air. It was amazing.

Mara, who was behind me, yelled, "Dahlia! Come here, look at what I found!"

"What?" I asked, running to her.

"A white moonflower—so cool, right?"

"Uh, what's a moonflower?"

"Oh, it's a flower that comes around Lunar Year and blooms on a full moon. It's pretty cool."

"Is it toxic?"

Before she could answer, she touched it and started playing with it.

"What are you doing? It could be dangerous!"

"Oh, please, there's nothing dangerous here. C'mon, touch it!"

"Um, okay."

Right after I touched it, we heard the teachers calling us to come back to the cabin. And as I was running back, I felt a little weird—like I wanted to faint or something.

While we were in our cabin, I was chatting with my friends, and that's when I realized I had to take my heat control meds. But I didn't want just to say, *"Guys, I gotta take my meds,"* because that would be weird—they already think I'm weird. And I didn't want anyone to know I had a big health problem. I mean, I know they know about it, but it was better if I just kept it to myself.

After five minutes, I was turning red.

"Dahlia, are you okay? You look like you're boiling," Lizzie asked.

"Yeah, you're turning red," Emily added.

"Uh, yeah, I'm fine, I just…"

Mara interrupted and said, "You just need to take your meds or something?"

"What?" I asked, feeling light-headed already rising.

"You know, your enzyme problem?"

"Oh my Gosh! You're doing it again! Guys, how many times do I have to tell you, I'm fi—"

Before I could finish my sentence, my eyes just closed. Like, I went blind. I could still hear people's voices, but I couldn't open my eyes. My enzymes started reacting and went high. It was like my life flashed before my eyes…

CHAPTER 10

When I woke up, I saw a girl sitting on a chair, looking worried.

"Oh my Gosh, Dahlia, you're awake!"

"Mara? Wha–what's going on? Where am I?" I asked.

"Um, in a hospital."

"What? What do you mean, hospital? What happened to me?!"

"You fainted last night in the cabin while we were chatting."

"Fainted? How did I faint?"

"I don't know. I guess it had something to do with your enzyme problem."

"What? But that only happens when I'm overheating or when I get bad reactions from my body. And where's Lizzie and Emily?"

The thing is, I knew exactly how my body acted up, but I didn't know why it acted so quickly.

"They didn't come. Everyone is still in the woods. We brought you to the hospital because you weren't waking up, and we didn't have anything to make you wake up."

"I'm so confused. You mean we're not in the woods, but in a hospital in the middle of nowhere?"

"No. We're back in Miami. The doctors are just checking up on you to see if you're okay to go back to the woods."

"And if I'm not?"

"I guess you'll be going back home." She shrugged like nothing was wrong with me right now.

"What? I can't go back home! I actually enjoy being in the woods. And I don't just faint because of my health issue!"

A doctor then entered the room and checked my IV.

"Hi... you're Dahlia, right?" the doctor asked.

"Yeah," I answered.

"Well, I'm Dr. Harman, and I'm here to check on your health issues and results."

"Is it okay? Can I still go back to the woods?"

"Well... unfortunately, no. Your BP were really high and getting out of control. It seems to be a plant that's causing the issue."

"What? What do you mean by a plant?"

"Did you touch any plants around? Like toxic ones?"

"Uh, I'm not sure about toxic plants, but I did touch a flower."

Dr. crossed his arms and tilted his head. "What flower, may I ask?"

"Uh, a moonflower, I think."

"Wow... Dahlia, that's a very dangerous flower. It could have killed you by now!"

"What? But Mara said it wasn't dangerous!" I looked at Mara, and she acted like she didn't know anything I was saying.

"Okay, well, dangerous or not, your blood is still not doing well. That means you'll be staying in this hospital until you're well—at least for a day or two."

"Why? Can't I stay at home or something?"

"Dahlia, your body is already not good enough, so touching a dangerous flower makes it worse. It could cause irritation, nausea, or fainting. The best thing we can do is let you stay here for a while till you're good enough."

"Doctor, please, I can't stay here. My parents will kill me if they find out."

"Well, we already called your parents, and they should be here by now." He checked his watch.

"What? No! They're gonna make me be homeschooled again, and then I can't meet my friends!"

I rose from the bed, but as I said that, I thought about it and realized I didn't have any friends. My real friends wouldn't be back in the woods relaxing while they knew I was in danger. They knew all about me being homeschooled and my parents worrying too much about me.

At some point, I thought they cared. But I guess I'll never have good friends. Maybe I never did anyway.

CHAPTER 11

It was 11:30 a.m. when I was brought to the hospital; now it's noon, and my parents have finally come—and they brought my sister. But they looked really worried.

"Dahlia! Oh my gosh, are you okay?" Mom said, rushing to my side.

"We were worried you wouldn't last five minutes in that forest," Dad added.

"It's okay, I'm fine. I just… I just fainted, that's all."

"Just fainted? Honey, you're burning up! Did you even take your meds with you to the woods?" She slowly touched my cheeks, her eyes roaming around my body.

I hesitated to talk. This was never a good idea. "Uh—"

"The doctor just told us before we came here that it was a flower that caused all this, and you weren't following your health protocols?" Dad said, cutting me off.

"Okay, okay, you wanna know everything? Fine. Today, the principal allowed us to go for a walk in the forest. Then one of my friends called me to come look at a flower, which was called a moonflower, and I didn't know it was dangerous. I didn't know anything in the woods was dangerous, so I touched it. At first, I didn't really care about it, but then, in our cabin, I started turning red. Even though I knew I was overheating, I didn't get the chance to take my meds, and I fainted. That's what happened."

My whole family was startled when I said that. I blinked rapidly, still surprised this even happened.

"Dahlia! That's way too extreme! Do you know how weak your body is right now? It's trying its best to heal up and be strong, but you just had to be dumb and touch that flower!" Mom yelled.

And that's when I realized—I messed up. Really badly. I knew I wasn't going to have a good day now.

"We are going back home, and you're not to leave the house unless you have our permission and we agree," Mom said firmly.

"What? No, Mom, you can't do that!"

"Oh yes, I can. According to discipline, your dad and I can decide how to treat you well!"

Mom quickly left the room, holding Olivia's hand tightly in hers.

Dad folded his arms. "The doctor may have said one or two nights here, but once you're discharged, we're in charge. And at home, you'll follow our rules."

CHAPTER 12

Two days later, after endless checkups and questions, the doctor finally let me go. When we reached home, I ran straight to my room before anything else could happen. But before I could open my door, Mom shouted, "Where do you think you're going?!"

I answered with an angry face. "Uh, to my room? Since I can't even go out!"

I slammed the door, sat on my bed, took out my phone, and called Mara. It wasn't the right thing to do right now, but I was sure talking to Mara would've kind of helped.

"Hey," Mara answered, waving slowly through the camera.

"Hi. Terrible day, huh?" I sighed, a soft breath escaping me.

"Yeah. Are you okay, though?"

"Yeah, I'm fine for now. I probably can't go to school anymore because of this."

She sighed in misery. "Well... I guess I'm the reason why you're in trouble right now."

"Who said? It's not your fault, okay? It's just my parents being so annoying and stressed about my health. Even though I'm okay right now."

I didn't really mean that. Mara and her friends kind of pushed me to the limit—if that even makes sense. But I knew they had little care for me. Apart from my health problem, they really didn't care.

"Great—oh, by the way, I'm sorry about the flower. I didn't know it was dangerous. My grandma told me she used to play with it all the time when she was young, so I thought—"

"Mara, it's okay. It didn't really cause many problems, just a little body heat. But apart from that, I'm okay."

"Really? Great! Because I thought you'd be angry at me."

"Maybe a little bit upset, but you're my only first friend. I can't be angry at you."

She chuckled. "Thanks. Um, I gotta go now—text you later."

"Alright, bye."

After that call, Mom called me downstairs for a "talk," and I knew it was going to be about the forest accident. When I sat at the dinner table, Olivia came to me holding a bowl of chocolate chip cookies.

"What's this for?" I asked.

"For you! You know, because your body has been flaring up since…"

I was really shocked at that point. Why would she think cookies would solve this problem?

I turned to my parents and asked, "Mom, Dad, are you serious? Is this how you're gonna treat me now? How many times do I have to tell this world—I'm fine!"

"Dahlia! Please, listen—"

I interrupted Mom. "No, you listen—all of you. I'm fine, I'm okay. I don't need your guidance or worries. As you can see, I'm living, breathing well, and I came out of that hospital well and okay. Why can't you get that?"

Mom looked like she was about to cry and said, "Honey, we do understand it, okay? It's just…"

"It's just what? You can't trust me? That I'll be fine? It was just an accident—it wasn't that bad. Why can't you just let it go?!"

Dad interrupted me and yelled, "Alright, that's enough, Dahlia! You can't just keep trying to convince us—it's not going to work!"

He sighed, and I cooled down a little.

"Like your mom said, we get it, we really do. It's just that we can't trust your blood vessels or heart. Anytime we go for an appointment to check your body, it's always bad news. It's barely ever good news."

"But at my last appointment, Dr. Donach said my enzymes were getting okay and that I could start school."

"Yeah, but not for long," Mom muttered.

"Huh? What do you mean?"

"You're not going to that school anymore, Dahlia. We'll probably start homeschooling again. I think that's better for your health." Mom crossed her arms.

"What? No way! First, you make me stay home every day and not go out, and now you're making me be homeschooled again?"

"I'm really sorry, Dahlia, but it's the only choice—just to make sure you don't get another injury from your disease."

"No, it's not! You're just ruining my life, not making it better—not even a little bit!"

Olivia slowly put the cookies down and said, "Dahlia—"

I interrupted her and continued, "My whole life, I've been sick, never getting better. I had to fly all the way to New York just to get surgery, and that barely helped me! And now you're making me stay home all day getting homeschooled?!"

That was the first time I ever yelled at my parents that long. I saw tears drop from Mom's eyes, and Dad looked really upset. Then Olivia started crying loudly. She ran to her room and locked the door.

It felt like I yelled at my own little sister, even though I really didn't—I was just trying to say 'I'm fine' to my parents. But harshly, I guess.

"Olivia!" Mom shouted.

I ran to her room and knocked. "Olivia, please open the door—it's really dangerous locking yourself in a room."

I could still hear her crying. I tried a hack on the door I found on the internet—and it worked.

I entered and sat beside her.

"Hey, it's gonna be okay. Mom and Dad are just overreacting. They always do that, you know?"

She wiped her tears and said, "Why, though? I mean, I get it, but why can't they just make our lives better?"

"Honestly, I don't know. I think every parent does that."

"So it's normal? It's normal for your parents to worry so much about you?"

"Um, I guess? I mean, I've kinda gotten used to it, but sometimes it drives me crazy."

"Yeah, but everything will be alright. They'll change, right?"

"Um, I can't promise you they'll change, but I'm sure everything will be alright."

I hugged her and kissed her on the forehead.

That was when Mom and Dad stepped into the room. They sat beside us, their voices steady, as they began to unravel everything they had been carrying—what worried them, why it weighed so heavily, and why they believed it should matter to me.

And in that moment, I found myself beginning to understand.

It happened so quickly, like they'd been waiting for a moment like this to finally talk about it.

"So, you don't actually wanna be worried?" I asked.

Mom sighed and answered, "No, but... I guess that's the way parents show they care, even if it's over the top."

So I was right—but now I kind of feel bad.

"I'm sorry. I'm sorry I've been hard on you guys. I didn't know because I didn't understand. Everyone has been worried about me because I might die and stuff."

They all nodded.

"But... why? I'm fine, though. And I don't think I'll die yet," I added.

"Well, we don't know for sure if you are gonna die—just maybe… we don't know how long you'll last in this world. But having fun with you, and protecting you, is what we should be doing together," Mom smiled.

Olivia got up and started jumping happily. "When you mean 'having fun together,' does that mean we can go to Disney World?!"

"Uh, I'm not sure—" Dad started, but Mom interrupted him and said,

"Actually, yeah, we can. We're gonna have fun… as a family, with no worries."

She winked at Dad, and for the first time in what felt like forever, happiness settled over me—without stress, without sadness, without worry attaching itself to me from every side.

And in that moment, surrounded by my family, I felt a closeness I had never known before. Maybe I had never understood it in the past, but sitting there, I finally did.

IT WAS NEVER JUST SUMMER

"Some words stay longer than the people

who said them."

CHAPTER 1

Living in Dartmouth, Nova Scotia, always felt a little intimidating—quiet streets, misty mornings, and way too many trees that made everything feel like it was hiding something. This morning started like any other: same heavy backpack, same cracked sidewalk under my shoes, same slow walk to school with music playing low in one ear.

But halfway down my usual street, I heard it—quick, heavy footsteps right behind me. Not just a shuffle or some echo. Actual steps.

I paused, turned my head fast, ready to face someone, something... but the sidewalk behind me was completely empty. No one there. Just silence, like the sound had never existed. But I know what I heard.

The second I stepped into school—still half freaked out from this morning—I went straight to my friends to tell them.

"Hold on—footsteps? Like, behind you?" Jessie blinked, then cracked up.

I raised a brow. "What's so funny?"

Jessie could barely speak through her laughter. "Girl, how does something like that even happen?"

"Imagining things again?" Celia said with a grin, leaning over like she already knew I was crazy.

I froze. Rude. They still acted like I had some brain issue or whatever—and I've told them a million times, I don't. But sure, laugh it up.

I wanted to talk more about it with them, even though they wouldn't really agree, but just as class started, Mrs. Johnson walked in with someone unfamiliar behind her.

"Everyone, this is Kyung. He's our new student, here on scholarship from South Korea."

Gasps echoed through the room, and yeah... I joined in.

They said he'd been awarded scholarships from programs all over the world, and somehow, he'd chosen to land here.

And okay—he's kinda cute. But no. We're not doing that.

His appearance wasn't easy to ignore: though he had light blond hair draping over his face and back. You could only see half of his eyes, and his lips tied it all together—a soft, light pink that matched the rest of his pale look. He was wearing a white long-sleeved shirt with a long black tie. One sleeve was rolled up, and his pants were just black—but cute.

It wasn't exactly the last day of school, though it felt like it. We were in the final stretch—the last week, only a handful of days left before summer. Most of the teachers had already stopped giving out lessons, trading them in for review games or long talks about next year.

So when he walked in, it didn't feel as strange as it should have. Sure, he wasn't here to learn equations or grammar rules, but at least he'd get to meet us before everything ended. A late start, maybe—but not too late to matter. And honestly, the timing only made his arrival stand out more.

CHAPTER 2

But when the bell rang, everybody headed out quickly. I never realized people cared so much about their next classes—but since it's the last week, they do.

"Wow, a lot of people really are going to enjoy summer break soon…" Jess said, stretching her arms over her head as we walked.

I didn't think she meant to bring up summer break so quickly, since the bell hadn't even rung for us to go home yet.

"So?" I replied, adjusting the strap of my bag.

"You know I have a bunch of Zoom classes and assignments to finish, right?" she added, pulling out her phone to double-check something.

"Yeah?" Celia asked, glancing over Jess's shoulder.

"Well, the file got deleted," she groaned, "and now my professor doubled the work. I might not even get to enjoy the break."

"You still can," I said, stepping around a backpack someone had left in the middle of the hall. "I mean, summer's like three months long. I doubt you're gonna spend all of it locked in your room doing assignments."

"Exactly," Celia added, nudging her with a grin. "And we're your best friends. We're not about to let you have a miserable break, trust me."

"Thanks, guys," Jessie said softly, hugging us both as we paused at the corner.

The hallway buzzed louder as the next period loomed, and students began peeling off in different directions. Jessie let go of us with a sigh, tucking her phone back into her pocket.

"Guess this is my stop," she said, heading toward her math class. Celia and I exchanged a quick smile before parting ways, too. The day wasn't over yet, though.

By the time the final bell rang, the classrooms had emptied into a flood of voices and footsteps rushing for the doors. The air felt lighter, like the whole building had been waiting for summer to finally arrive. I slipped out with the crowd, spotting Jessie and Celia near the gates, and together we started the walk home.

We split ways quickly, since we live kind of close to each other. Jessie reached her house first, waving before disappearing through the front door. Celia followed soon after, leaving me to walk the last stretch alone.

"Great, now I'm alone," I muttered, kicking a tiny rock ahead of me.

But just a few steps later, I slowed down. Someone walking up ahead looked kind of familiar.

I squinted.

Wait… was that Caelum?

It was strange that he was still walking home after all this time. And the fact that he was going to Havenbrook Hill—that street is mainly for rich people. He must be rich to live in such a neighborhood.

And how did I know he was rich? The tutors, travels, training, and special help he gets in class tell me in my mind that only someone with money could pull that off.

I'd also heard his dad was the CEO of Clean First (the first and apparently neatest cleaning company in Canada). Then he must be a neat person.

I was about ten feet away from him and his friends, and I didn't think they noticed me, but I heard most of what they were talking about.

"Man, I wish I could go surfing. It's my first and last thing to do this summer," one of his friends said.

"Don't worry—there's still one chance you can go and drown in the ocean while surfing," Caelum said sarcastically.

His other friend started laughing. It wasn't even funny—it was rude. I couldn't keep listening to all the things he was saying to that poor guy, who I think is in my Social Studies class. Maybe both of them are.

But then I got so angry at what he was saying that I lost my temper and groaned.

Caelum heard me and turned around. "Uh… what are you doing?"

I couldn't be more embarrassed, so I said something I thought was smart.

"Uhh… going home. What else?"

"It sure didn't look like it. You're pretty close to even spying on me." He raised his eyebrows, crossing his arms as his friends stopped walking and waited for an answer. It was so awkward.

"Uh, n–no, I was trying to pass by, but you and your friends were blocking the way, so…"

Before anyone could say anything, I quickly walked past them and went home.

CHAPTER 3

When I reached, I went straight to my room without saying anything to my mom and shut the door. "Oh my god, that was so embarrassing!"

My mom heard me from downstairs and said, "Honey, are you okay?"

"Uh, yeah, I'm fine." I just hugged my puppy and started talking to him. Then I heard my phone ringing and picked it up—it was Jessie.

"Hey, Aliss!"

"Jessie, you wouldn't believe what happened!" I exclaimed, still embarrassed.

"What is it—wait, did you start your period?"

"What? No!" I started talking so fast about what happened, I was probably faster than Eminem's rapping songs.

"Okay, girl, chill. He's just a guy in our class. Maybe cute, but don't let him get in your head, okay? But… do you have a crush on him or something?"

"No!"

I ended the call, pressing the phone to my chest. "No, it's still in my head!" My thoughts twisted against me. *Maybe I do have a cru— no!*

"No way I'm into him. He's literally the new student, and… ew!"

The new week had started quietly—not with the rush of school mornings, but with the slower rhythm of home. No alarm buzzing, no scramble for books or bus rides—just sunlight slipping through the curtains and the comfort of knowing I didn't have to go anywhere. For once, the week wasn't about classrooms or crowded hallways. It was about being here, at home, where the hours belonged to me.

But I'm still thinking about what happened that day for some reason, and I'm awkwardly embarrassed.

When I went downstairs, I called my best friends to see if they wanted to go out for a bit. Luckily, they were both free the whole day today, so that was good.

"Hey, guys," I said to my girls when we got out on the street.

"Hey! I still can't believe my professor canceled my lessons today. I'm so lucky!" Jessie said, smiling.

"Yeah, good for you!" Celia said, holding Jessie's hand softly.

As the girls were talking, I was thinking of what to do during the summer break. Maybe convince my mom and me to go to the beach? Or fly somewhere for a vacation? New things to do with my mom are always fun... but I just didn't know exactly what to do. I mean, going out with my friends is fine, but it's going to get boring the more we do it, and I know they have other plans than just hanging out together.

When we reached a coffee shop, we decided to get something to drink before doing anything else. I ordered an iced mocha with boba pearls, and Celia ordered an iced pumpkin spice latte. As for Jessie, she ordered—well, had to order—an Apple Crisp Oat Milk Macchiato with ice cubes, plus a small box of five donuts and five cookies. Celia and I were just shocked.

"Jess, isn't that too much? You're probably going to get diabetes from that much sugar." Celia stared blankly at the treats.

Jessie scoffed and acted like it was no big deal. "It's fine, guys, no need to worry."

CHAPTER 4

When we finished, Jessie owed us some money from a carnival we went to and paid for all the food and rides. So instead of giving it to us, she decided to pay for our drinks—and boy, did she owe herself a lot of money! It cost her $40 for the food and drinks. But what happened next was even weirder.

I saw Caelum again. What is he doing here? Was he following me? He caught me, and I'm pretty sure he noticed I was staring—well, looking at him.

Caelum came close and leaned toward my face. "You better stop staring at me."

"I wasn't staring; I was looking at the menu," I said with a bit of hesitation.

"Really?" He was annoying me. Can't he just give up and leave? Like I just said—I wasn't looking at him.

"Which part of 'I wasn't looking at you' don't you understand?" I crossed my arms, looking bold. Luckily, he just sighed quietly and left. Then Celia started to give me looks, and I hated it.

"Ooh, Aliss, you have a crush…"

"Uh, no—I don't," I muttered under my breath.

"Oh, really?" Great, now Celia was annoying me. I really didn't think I had a crush on him.

"Yes. Now, please, stop." I rolled my eyes and sank into the chair. Even though Celia still wouldn't listen to me, I just ignored her little acts—the kind that were meant to get under my skin.

CHAPTER 5

After spending some time with my friends, we decided to go back home. It was 5:45 p.m., so I went to take a bath and then go for a walk. Alone.

I know it might be dangerous and unprotected, but since I'm sixteen, my mom allows me to do it—and many people drive around my neighborhood, so if something were to happen, everyone would notice.

As I was walking, I closed my eyes and started counting in my head. That's what I do when I walk or meditate; it helps me relax and calm my mind. But this time, I wasn't paying attention to where I was going and bumped into someone. The person caught me before I fell on them—and that person was… Caelum?

The question—*how many times am I going to meet him?*—made me wonder if, next time, I might accidentally kiss him.

"Whoa, watch it! Wait—Aliss?" Caelum said.

"Caelum?" I stared at him.

His eyes roamed all over me. "Are you okay?"

"Yeah, I'm fine. Sorry I hit you, I wasn't looking," I said, feeling a sharp ache in my head.

"Yeah, maybe you should get some glasses—or sense-is."

I don't know why I was meeting so many rude people this year. How could he say that?

"What? Or maybe *you* should get a new attitude!"

He snickered, his arms crossed but his gaze soft.

"Anyway, why are you walking on a dark, foggy night?" I asked, shaking my head.

"I should be asking you the same question." He slightly tilted his head.

"Well, I always go for a walk whenever I'm free at night."

"And I was just coming back from a party at my friend's house." He pointed to the street behind him—Bellbrook Crescent.

"Oh, are you going back home?"

"Yes. Are you? I mean—never mind." He shook his head, but I nodded.

"No, it's fine. I think I should. I feel dizzy anyway." I touched my head, feeling the burn.

"You are? Then let me take you."

Even though I didn't need help, I don't think I could walk back home—it was about seven to nine minutes away, and my whole-body kind of hurt.

"Okay," I agreed.

He then carried me and walked to my house. I smiled and was thankful for his kindness. To be honest, I'd thought of him as a rude guy, but...

When we reached my house, I got down, and he placed my hand on his shoulder so I wouldn't fall. I was still feeling dizzy, but it was touching how much he was helping me. He rang the doorbell, and Mom came out, surprised and confused.

"Oh, hello?"

"Hi, I'm Caelum, Aliss's classmate. Um, so Aliss was going for a walk, and she ran into me. Then she started feeling dizzy. I helped her get here, and I think she's still in pain."

I was so tired and sleepy that I couldn't see or hear properly what was happening.

When I woke up, I felt so… weird. It was morning, which meant I had slept through the entire evening. I got ready and went downstairs. I saw Mom in the backyard, gardening and watering the new plants and her gray birch.

"Hey, Mom."

"Oh, hey, honey! How was your sleep?" She stopped and turned to me.

"Oh, just… odd." I shrugged as my headache started to fade.

"Yeah, sorry—I gave you some medication for your head and body, but you'll be okay in no time."

"Med–medicine?" I raised both eyebrows.

"Yes. You don't remember?" I shook my head, and she told me the whole story from last night.

"Wait—so I felt tired and dizzy?"

"Yes, but it's gone now," Mom said with a small smile.

Since it was Saturday, I did my chores and then sat comfortably on the couch.

Cleaning was never my thing, but Mom always had a hard time keeping the place perfect since she never had a partner by her side.

Until I was about three, my dad used to live with us. But Mom never told me the whole story of what happened, so I always thought he left for "milk," like people say, or maybe they just got divorced. I never got too sad or devastated about it, but I used to overthink it. I'm just glad people never asked or bullied me about it—especially my friends.

And I love helping Mom, even though cleaning is the last thing I'd usually offer to help with.

"Ahh, now this is what I'm talking about!"

I opened my MG group chat and saw a lot of messages:

"Aliss, where are you?!"

"Omg, Aliss, are you dead?!"

"Aliss, please answer!"

I guess I hadn't texted anything in the group last night. I might as well call them. When I did, everyone immediately answered.

"Aliss, where have you been?!" Jessie cried out from the screen.

"Yeah, you didn't text or call us last night," Celia added.

"Uh, sorry guys, I felt dizzy last night and... and..."

"And?" Jessie cut me off.

"And Caelum carried me!"

Somehow, I shrieked like other teenagers would if a guy did that—but I didn't mean to.

"What?!" Celia said, shocked.

"Yeah, I was going for a walk when we randomly met, and I accidentally bumped my head on his chest," I explained.

"Aww," Jessie teased.

"Aliss, you know Jessie and I already have boys we're talking to, so *you* should get one—and Caelum is the one!" Celia shrieked.

I laughed with them and chatted for a while.

CHAPTER 6

After we finished talking, I went to my room and started writing in my diary, but I ended up falling asleep. Mom then came in later and was surprised to see me still dozing off.

"Aliss, wake up!"

"What happened?" I opened my eyes, yawning.

"Honey, you slept for three hours! What's going on? Are you okay?"

I slept for three hours. I know I sleep for a long time sometimes, but I've never slept for more than two hours.

"No, I'm okay. Maybe I was just so tired from doing chores for an hour," I said, giving Mom an annoyed look.

She chuckled and flicked her hand at me. "Oh, c'mon! It was just ten chores. I do more than that anyway!"

Then she left—just like that—not even giving me a forehead kiss or an *I love you*. But I don't blame her; she's always like that, unlike some moms who hug and give their kids candy for doing a lot of chores.

Anyway, I went to change my clothes and go for a walk—to exercise my body and get back its strength. But mostly, to say thank you to Caelum for helping me get home safely. Only if I saw him again… and luckily, I did.

"Caelum!" I called out his name.

"Hey!" He looked up from his phone and saw me turning from my street.

"What are you doing here, sitting on a bench?" I asked, putting my hands on my hips.

"Uh, I decided to take a break from learning in school—learning class today—and came here."

"Oh, okay. Shocking, we met again, huh?"

"Yeah. By the way, are you good from the pain last night?"

"Yeah, I'm good. What about you?"

He tilted his head, a bit confused.

"Well, I hit my big head on you, so—"

He chuckled. "Yeah, your head's so big, they might mistake it for a construction boulder."

"Wow, thanks for the compliment."

We both laughed at our jokes.

We kept talking, but somehow, we ended up just… staring at each other. Our eyes met and locked, and for a second, it felt weirdly cool—almost romantic. I didn't even know why. But I blinked it off and picked the conversation back up like nothing happened.

"Uh, anyway, I was calling you to say thank you for helping me get home."

"No worries," he smiled.

Then I said something embarrassing that almost ended our time right then.

"I don't know… there was something honest about it. It caught me off guard—in a good way," I said, my voice a little lower than usual. I waited for him to say something back—something just as thoughtful—but...

"Wait—did you think I was doing that because... I like you or something?"

"Well, yeah, I guess—"

He snickered and said something that made my smile disappear.

"No, Aliss, it's not like I like you. I took you home because I was doing a favor—to say sorry for you hitting my chest."

"Oh," I swallowed hard, looking down.

"I didn't expect you to think we're all of a sudden falling in love because of last night..."

I went quiet all of a sudden. I was starting to crush on him, to have feelings for him—but clearly, he didn't feel the same. It broke my heart that he kinda... rejected me.

CHAPTER 7

I went back home before anything worse happened, and after that night, I felt so stiff—like I couldn't move. It was all in my head, non-stop. The idea of talking to my best friends about this came to my mind, so I texted them and told them we should meet at the park the next morning.

"Hey, Aliss, so, what's up?" Jessie asked as we sat down on the bench.

"Something shocking happened last night. Again."

Then I explained everything to them and still felt heartbroken inside.

"Omg, Caelum is such a brat! I already realized it when he first came to school," Celia said, rolling her eyes, trying to blame him.

"Yeah, you didn't deserve it," Jessie added.

"No, you guys are just saying that because you want to make me feel better."

"Uh, no?" Jessie said.

"Why would we do that? We're your best friends, and you were the first person we talked to when we were new—until we became friends, and then best friends. Since ninth grade! That's three years now," Craise said, touching my shoulder.

"And we can't lie to you," Jessie added. "You never did, so why would we?"

It felt so heartwarming when they said that. I hugged them both, and somehow, after we hung out in the park, it made me smile again.

CHAPTER 8

Today was the first day of school, marking my third semester at Parkland High School. My best friends and I have been here for so long, and we're still here! I got ready as usual, wearing my white baggy shirt and black tight pants. My hair was pulled into two neat French braids—the kind that always made me look a little more put together than I felt. As they fell over my shoulders, the blonde highlights caught the light—faint, but noticeable. Closer to the roots, my natural brunette showed through. I never really loved the contrast, but I couldn't say I hated it either. It was just… me.

As I went downstairs, my mom surprised me with a great breakfast, and I was stunned.

"Good morning, honey," my mom smiled at me. She took a plate and dished out my breakfast.

"I made you your favourite—a strawberry pancake, a bowl of two different fruits, and a lemonade with a lemon slice on top of the glass."

It was beautiful, and it smelled and looked good. I knew my mom did this just to say, *"Have a great day at school."* And I was glad to have a mom like that.

"Omg, thanks, Mom!" I quickly dug in and surprisingly ate the whole dish. I got my backpack and said goodbye to her.

But as I was walking to school, I felt someone walking behind me. It was happening again—just like it did at the start last time. I immediately turned, and this time I saw Caelum.

Wait, so he was the one who disappeared when I first felt like someone was following me? Even though I was still angry about what he said last time, I didn't even say hi or look at him. I just turned my head before he could do anything and continued walking to school. He looked confused when I left, but that didn't make me feel sorry for him or anything, because he made me upset and ashamed that night during summer break.

"Okay, class, settle down! Welcome back to school. Some of you may not be happy, and some of you may be, but all I know is that you're gonna have a fun time today since it's a new term!" Mrs. Johnson exclaimed.

"So, who's excited?!"

The class stood up and started shouting happily—and geez, some people's squealing voices were crazy!

When school finished, I was pretty sad about it, but also happy, though. At least today, I wasn't done having fun; I was going to a carnival tonight.

My mom works at some carnivals around Canada, and since she has a pass and has been employed for this year, we can go today, or any day. Anyway, as I was happily hopping home, I bumped into someone I already knew from their shadow.

"Aliss," I sighed and turned to Caelum. He put his hands on his waist and looked worried about something.

"You've been ignoring me since summer break. What's going on? Are you angry at me? Did I do something wrong?"

"Did you do something? Hmm, let me think... yes, yes, you did!" I frowned.

"And want to know why I've been ignoring you?—wait, you should know, because you said it right in front of my face!"

Then he changed his expression from sad and confused to serious. "Is this about what I said to you last time we talked? Because if it is, I—I was just being honest, Aliss. Is it by force to like someone I don't want to like?" He was still being rude.

"No, I don't care if you don't like me—you're not even someone I would date anymore! It's just... how you said it. It made me feel humiliated. I already know you're a rude person, but sometimes it can hurt people. And because it's you saying it, you won't feel it, so... you wouldn't care."

Although I did care a little bit about his feelings for me, I looked down, still upset, and pushed him out of the way with tears in my eyes. It still pains me that he doesn't care about my feelings. And the fact that I liked him...

CHAPTER 9

When I reached home, Mom saw my sad face and asked, "Hey, Aliss, what's wrong? Why are you sad? Did something happen at school?"

I sat on the couch closest to me and lay on it.

"The only guy I've been talking to this year broke my heart."

Mom came and sat beside me, feeling sorry for me.

"Oh, honey, it must be a guy you like, huh?"

I nodded, hoping Mom would just leave me to be alone, though.

"Okay, since you're sad and broken-hearted, maybe…" She sighed, and I looked at her.

"We won't have to go to the carnival tonight, if you like."

I smiled a little. I was glad my mom knew what was wrong with me and left me be.

"Thanks, Mom," I said, going to bed tired, but still crying out my sad feelings. I hoped the next day would be better.

The next day wasn't any different. I kept ignoring Caelum, and—oddly enough—his not trying anymore made it worse. That's how you know the trust's gone: when silence feels heavier than the arguments. But before I could spiral too deep into it, Celia and Jessie showed up at my table in the cafeteria.

"Hey, Aliss—hold up, what's wrong?" Jessie asked curiously.

I couldn't even talk; I was so angry at myself and Caelum. Then I heard Celia whisper something to Jessie, and she nodded.

"We'll see you later, Aliss," Jessie muttered.

I honestly didn't know why they left. Maybe it was because they thought I needed a break and some time alone? Or maybe they thought I needed to think about my feelings and how Caelum hurt me? I actually didn't know if that was why.

School ended with the kind of sunset that made everything feel still—soft streaks of gold and orange painting the sky. I couldn't stop looking at it. But then I felt a hand on my shoulder. I didn't even have to turn around—I already knew it was him. Caelum.

And honestly, the nerve. He had no right to think he could just walk up to me like we were still friends. Like I'd talk to him. Like I'd forgive him.

But I still had something to say.

"Seriously, what do you want now? Can't you just leave a girl alone for about... a day?!"

"No, because we need to talk," he said, his expression unreadable.

Before I could respond, he gently took my hand and led me toward a nearby building. I didn't know what was going on, but I didn't pull away either. We climbed the stairs—floor after floor—until we reached the roof.

CHAPTER 10

The view was stunning. The city below shimmered under the last light of the day, and the sunset bathed everything in this quiet, golden glow. I could feel the silence starting to stretch between us, so I broke it first.

"So, why did you bring me here?"

"I know you have a lot of questions, so I'm ready to answer," he muttered. He was right—I wanted to ask him some things.

"Okay, firstly, are you this rude all the time?"

"Actually, no. I'm not," he said quietly. "I used to be this kind, chill guy back in Korea, but… that changed when my mom died. I had just turned sixteen." His voice wavered, and he sniffled, trying to keep it together.

"My dad didn't care. Not even a little. He moved on so fast, as if she were just a memory. I couldn't even look at him anymore. Then he thought moving to Canada would somehow fix everything—make me happy again. But…"

I froze. I had no idea he'd been carrying all that. And the way I treated him lately? I was too harsh. Way too harsh.

"I'm… I'm so sorry about that. You've been going through a hard time, and I didn't even bother to ask what was wrong."

"No, it's fine, I understand. You didn't know."

I still felt bad for him, but it didn't mean he had to be so rude to people.

"You can ask another if you want," he said as he cleared his throat.

"Okay, uh—" I kept thinking about it for a while before I asked, "Do you... do you actually not like me?"

He turned to me, his eyes meeting mine with a seriousness that made my heart race. For a second, I braced myself, thinking he was about to say something embarrassing.

"You know what? I'll just be honest," he said, his voice steady.

"Aliss, you're one of the most genuine, stunning people I've met. The girls in our class... they don't compare. And the reason I said I didn't like you? I was afraid. Afraid you'd reject me. I've never had to deal with that before. I've never been heartbroken—apart from my mom—but you're different, and I actually care about you."

I stared at him, eyebrows lifting in surprise. He really thought someone like me would reject someone like him? It almost felt ironic.

"That's why I kept finding excuses to bump into you. I couldn't stop thinking about you," he added, more quietly this time.

My chest tightened. I had no idea he felt all of that—especially before I even realized how I felt.

"So all this time... you were acting distant because you liked me?" I asked.

He gave a small shrug. "Yeah. Pretty much."

My face was burning now, a deep blush rushing in. "I... I like you too."

Then, without another word, we kissed. It wasn't perfect or planned, but it felt right. And for a moment, the world paused, just for us.

SHAUNA'S STAND-UP

"Comedy doesn't need age; it can belong to a child just as much as an adult.

CHAPTER 1

"**W**ho's a girl who loves making funny jokes and wants to be a stand-up comedian?"

Well, if you haven't guessed, it's me.

Some people dream about being rock stars or actors. Me? I just want to make people laugh until their stomachs hurt. I'm half British, half Irish, and fully obsessed with comedy. Ever since I was five, I've been practicing punchlines like they were math problems—only way more fun. And if I'm lucky, one day the world will know me as *the* Shauna Williams, best known for my jokes instead of just my messy handwriting.

Anyway, today I was in the bathroom taking a shower when my older brother, Aaron, started knocking on the door.

"Aren't you done already?" he called out.

"No, give me a sec!" I yelled back.

"Well, hurry, doofus! I don't wanna be late to school!"

I quickly wrapped a towel around my body and went to my room. And if you heard my brother, yes—we're going to school. You might think it's not a big deal, but for me, it is. I have a serious test today. It's a math test. And let me tell you something: I'm not good at math. Never in my whole life have I been good at math. And tests are even worse! I knew for sure I was going to fail anyway…

"Kids, you'd better come down before your food gets cold, because I'm not cooking another plate for you!" my mom yelled from the kitchen.

I jogged downstairs to the table to see a delicious English breakfast, smelling sweet and savory.

"Mmm, grilled tomatoes, crispy hash browns, and sausages! Thanks, Mom." I smiled and sat down.

"Where's your brother?" Mom asked, cutting veggies at the table.

As soon as I was about to answer, Aaron came downstairs in his school uniform, looking like a gangster who lives in the hood.

He sat on the counter stool and said, "Sup." I don't know if he was saying hi to me or all of us.

"Oh my gosh, Aaron! What is this ugly, disgusting outfit you're wearing?" Mom exclaimed.

"Relax," Aaron said, leaning on the counter. "It's my school uniform."

"That you changed into some ugly, broke-assassin fit?" I joked.

Aaron and I laughed, but Mom wasn't having it.

"Okay, that's enough of the jokes, both of you."

"Yeah, stop with the act," Dad said as he came in. "Finish your breakfast and get to school. The bus is almost here."

We quickly ate our breakfast, put on our jackets and boots, and went to the school bus.

CHAPTER 2

Ten minutes later, the bus finally came. I got on and went to the back to meet my friend, Martin—the only friend I've had since school started.

"Hey," I waved and sat down.

"Hi," he smiled.

"So, did you get the news from the school that they're bringing clubs?" he asked.

"Clubs? What do you mean?" I tilted my head.

"Like extracurricular activities. Your parents should've gotten the message."

"Oh yeah, I actually can't believe they did that. I never knew the school would be into those things."

"Mhm, but are you planning on joining one?"

"Mm, I don't know… maybe. Are you?"

"I think so. My parents—Mom especially—would lecture me about joining anyway."

"Oh, okay."

After that talk, we reached Parkland High and went straight to our classes. My first period was Art. I sat in the middle of the class, next to a blonde girl.

"Okay, class," the teacher began, "today we're starting our Cultural Art project. By that, I mean creating art based on traditions—where you come from, your heritage, your background."

It looked and sounded pretty easy, but it wasn't for me. Even though I'm British and Irish, it was still hard to figure out how my background was made from two countries—Britain and Ireland. It was supposed to be about our culture and traditions, but I didn't know much about Ireland—maybe a little about Britain, since they teach us here—but my parents wouldn't even tell me a single thing about their country, except the food.

"Hey," the girl next to me whispered.

I turned to her. "Yeah?"

"Do you understand the art topic?"

"Uh, kind of. But I'm half British, half Irish, so I don't know much about traditions and cultures."

"Oh my gosh, same!" she said, covering her mouth in shock.

"Wait, you're Irish and British too?"

"No, I'm British, but my great-great-great-grandparents were even in World War II."

It kind of sounded like a joke, which gave me an idea.

"Oh wow. Well, I have a joke about it."

"What is it?"

I know I barely knew this girl, but she looked cool—and okay to tell my jokes to.

"It's not really about the natives, but… 'My father is a bus driver who circles Big Ben in London; he works around the clock.'"

She made a whisper-laugh, which made it even funnier. And actually, that's my dad's profession.

"Gosh, stop—that's actually kind of funny! 'Clock,' that's a good one."

I smiled happily, because this was the first time a random stranger had ever laughed at my jokes (aside from my brother and Martin).

CHAPTER 3

A nyway, at our last gym class, Mrs. Davison, our coach, decided to let us do whatever we wanted.

"I guess it's a free period then," Martin said, resting his hands on his knees.

"Yeah," I copied him.

"Wanna just sit and watch the class do stupid things or play something?"

"Um—" Before Martin could answer, the same girl from earlier came running toward us.

"Hey!"

"Um… hi, do we know you?" Martin asked, looking into her dark green eyes.

"I'm Dietra, from Arts and Spanish class."

"Oh! So you're that girl I was sitting next to when I told that joke!" I chuckled under my breath.

"Yeah! I'll be honest, that was the first time I've ever heard such a cool joke like that," she smiled.

"So you guys already know each other?" Martin asked, glancing at both of us.

"Yeah," I said.

"So… want to play tag or something?" Dietra asked.

"Sure!" I stood up straight.

We looked at Martin, hoping he'd join us, but before anything could happen, he touched Dietra's shoulder and said, "Tag! You're it!" Then he ran all the way to the end of the gym. I knew I had to run before Dietra could tag me.

Later on, I noticed she was only trying to tag Martin. I was kind of confused for a second—until Martin got tagged and ran straight toward me.

"Aaah!" I yelled, running away from him, and he tagged me right as the bell rang.

"Alright, everyone," Coach Davison said. "Time to head home."

I stopped running and went out the gym door.

"Why'd you keep running?" Martin said, panting.

"I don't know. What did you expect me to do—crawl? Walk?"

He laughed. "Okay, whatever. Let's get home."

While we were taking our things out of the locker, Dietra came over with her backpack and sports bag.

"What's that for?" I asked.

"Oh, I'm going to a basketball class," Dietra said.

"Wow, didn't know you liked basketball," Martin smiled.

"Well, I do. See you tomorrow. Bye!"

Martin and I waved.

"So… should we go?" he said, grabbing his backpack.

"Mhm. Is your aunt picking us up?"

"Uh, she's out of town, so walking it is. By the way, where's your brother?"

"Oh, he comes home like five or ten minutes later."

Since school was pretty far from home, we walked and got there in fifteen minutes. I said goodbye to Martin and went inside the house.

CHAPTER 4

Mom was in the kitchen making a call, and Dad was on the couch watching TV.

"Hey, Dad," I said, walking up to him.

"Oh, hey, kiddo!" He turned to me, smiling. "How was school?"

"Good."

I hugged him and went to eat dinner. I was having rice and chicken, and then Aaron finally came home.

That same night, I was in my room at my desk, writing comedy jokes. That's something I started doing last year—getting a piece of paper and writing random, cool, different jokes. Mostly to tell people and see if they think it's funny.

Like I said in the beginning, I really want to be a comedian. But I can't be successful at it unless my parents agree. And without their support, I don't think I'll ever be great in comedy.

Anyway, I had to stop writing because it was almost my bedtime.

The next day at school, I was getting my books from my locker when I was surprised by my two friends, Martin and Dietra, with some shocking news.

"Shauna!" Dietra smiled so happily.

"Uh… what's up?" I muttered, confused.

"We've got some great news." Martin leaned against my locker.

"The school has finally announced that they're bringing clubs!" Dietra said.

"Yeah, I know," I nodded.

"Well, did you know they're bringing clubs like a comedy club?"

I raised both my eyebrows in shock. "Uh, no—wait, are they really?"

"Yeah!"

"And you could join—especially since you're such a funny girl," Martin said with a smile.

I stammered in hesitation.

"Oh, c'mon! Don't say no, you have to join! You could learn great jokes and make your comedian life better!" Dietra exclaimed.

"I–I don't know… If it's an after-school club, I can't join because my mom will want me home before 3:30, and I know my parents wouldn't agree anyway." I frowned.

Martin sighed in disbelief while Dietra tried to back me up.

"Don't worry," she said, touching my shoulder. "It'll be fine. I know you want to join, and if we have to confront and try to convince your parents to agree, we will."

I smiled and said, "Thanks, Dietra."

But I know my parents—there's nothing anyone can do to make them change their minds…

CHAPTER 5

As soon as school ended, Martin and Dietra were waiting for me by a random classroom door in the hallway. I walked up to them with a muddled expression.

"What's going on now?"

Dietra had this bright look on her face, which made me even more confused—but also a bit excited.

"Shauna... I know you'll probably not agree with this, but the comedy club just started today, and I was hoping you'd join now!"

"Me?" I pointed to myself.

"Yeah! We told them how funny and great you are at comedy and thought you could join the club. There, you could learn more jokes and stuff, you know."

"But I told you, my parents wouldn't—"

"We know, we know," Martin cut in. "They'd disagree. But this is once in a lifetime. I'm not sure you'll ever get this opportunity again. Forget about your parents for now; eventually, we'll tell them."

For some reason, I had a genuine smile on my face. "Alright, I'll join. But just because you guys said so."

Martin nodded, and Dietra opened the door for me to enter.

As I walked in, a sudden rush ran through me—a shiver that left goosebumps on my arms—and all I wanted was to get out. Everyone's eyes turned toward me as the teacher welcomed me in. I slipped into a seat beside a tall girl with brown pigtails, and immediately, I caught her body odor. It wasn't deadly, but let's just say deodorant should've been her best friend.

But it wasn't a problem at all. The teacher had already finished a topic before I came in, and now continued talking about how comedy works. Surprisingly, I already understood it. It was like I'd known it all along. I guess watching popular comedians like Dave Chappelle on YouTube really paid off.

Mrs. Colleen then smiled and wrapped up her talk. "Okay, FCs— Future Comedians—that's it for today. Please pack up your things and head home."

That's it? That's all the information we had to learn about comedy? It only lasted about five minutes. I wanted to ask the teacher more about the comedy club, since the topic ended so quickly, but eventually, everyone started leaving—even the teacher. So I had to go too.

CHAPTER 6

S o I went outside the school building, where my friends were waiting for me, and I told them all about it.

"Wow…" Dietra raised both eyebrows.

"Well, that's weird," Martin muttered.

"Yeah! Weird for a beginner comedian to join a club thinking it would help improve their jokes and stuff—but instead, it failed." I scoffed.

Dietra shrugged. "Uh… I wouldn't say it was a fail since you just started—and you came late. Maybe you should give it another chance. It's worth a shot."

"A chance? Hello? Middle school is almost over! I'm about to graduate and go to high school. I shouldn't be waiting to give anything a chance—it's too late."

"Oh, c'mon, Shauna, don't give up just like that. You're going to be a better comedian than you think. You just have to… try." Martin tried to convince me.

I thought about it for a minute. "Fine," I sighed. "I'll give it another try. Maybe I can learn more and get better at comedy."

"Now that's what I'm talking about!" Dietra smiled and clapped for a second. But honestly, I still thought it was best to just stay home and learn comedy from YouTube.

When I got home, it was already late, so I knew I was in trouble.

"Where have you been?" Mom asked, finishing her work on the computer.

"Um, at school? Like always." Don't ask why I was even trying to be smart.

"School? School ends at 3:00. You're coming home at 3:25—and even your brother came earlier." She glanced at her small brown Rolex watch.

"Well, there was a school meeting, and we had to stay for an extra twenty-five minutes."

"And what was the meeting about?" Mom got up from the computer table.

"Um… about student behavior?" I shrugged nervously, hoping she wouldn't find anything suspicious.

"Oh, behavior? Well, your behavior right now isn't helping the fact that you're lying!" She put her hands on her hips, waiting for me to answer. At that point, I just had to tell the truth.

"Okay, okay, fine. I'll tell the truth," I sighed, sitting down at the dining table.

"Well?" Mom pressed.

"Today, my friends told me about new clubs that are coming to the school. Well, they're actually activities we can join. So, after school today, my friends convinced me to join… the comedy club."

Mom's face froze in shock.

"Oh, a comedy club? But the news I got from the school was about clubs that could help you improve your skills in whatever you're best at."

"Yeah—and comedy is what I'm best at."

"But I thought we agreed that you wouldn't be a comedian or do anything related to comedy." She tilted her head and leaned closer.

"But Mom, you know I'm good at comedy! You know I love it—and I want to be a great comedian in the future!"

"Shauna, we talked about this. No child of mine shall say, 'I want to be a comedian.' It will not happen in my house!"

"Mom, you can't do that! I've been doing comedy since I was five, and now that you think comedy is stupid, you never let me do it! Even though I decide to be and do what I want—"

"Enough!" Mom yelled loudly, then continued in a firm voice. "You know exactly why you can't do comedy. I realized comedy was stupid because of a good reason."

I scoffed, knowing full well that comedy isn't stupid.

"From now on, I don't want to hear or see that you're doing comedy again. Because if I do… you know what's going to happen."

Mom then stepped back a bit and forced a smile.

"You know I'm just trying to make your life better—in fact, your future life better. And comedy isn't going to help. It's a waste of time and stupid jokes."

I whined and walked away from her side.

CHAPTER 7

Angrily barging into my room, I noticed Aaron was in the living room, watching a car race on the television with Dad. "Hey, doofus," Aaron looked at me. "Where have you been?"

I ignored him and quickly went to my room. I flopped on the bed and lay on my tummy.

Since I started doing comedy, I still don't understand why Mom—and Dad—won't let me do what I love. And what Mom meant by *"you know what's going to happen"* was that everybody who knows me also knows how bad I am in school—especially in subjects like Math and Science.

Like I said in the beginning, when it comes to any math test, there's a 99% chance I'll fail. And when my parents found out I got D's and F's on my report card last semester, they decided I'd start taking school learning classes on Zoom.

You'd probably think that's not so bad—but the worst part is that it's **every single day**, from 3:10 to 7:00 p.m.!

So, anytime I come back from school, after dinner, I have to quickly go on the computer and start the meeting. And I don't want to pressure myself like that. My parents just don't understand how much I love making jokes and making people laugh. I help people forget their sadness and smile for a moment. But I also don't want to disrespect my mom or ignore her rules.

Anyway, I was so tired from the day that I stopped thinking about the comedy issue, closed my eyes, and fell asleep immediately.

However, the next morning, I was still in a bad mood. I finished getting ready in five minutes instead of my usual ten to fifteen.

I jogged downstairs and saw a bowl of porridge waiting for me.

"Really, Mom? Porridge?" I gave the food a disgusted look.

"Yes, it's good for you. You need protein and fiber in your body."

I still didn't want to eat it, but Mom gave me that serious look that made it impossible to resist.

"So, Shauna," Dad said from across the counter. "Your mom told me you've started doing comedy again."

I sighed, sounding annoyed.

"Care to explain that?"

I ignored him and kept eating my porridge, but then Mom mumbled under her breath,

"She's just being disobedient."

"Mom!" I frowned and yelled. "You have no right to say that! I love comedy, and I started when I was literally born! You can't just ..."

"That's enough!" Dad yelled back. "Don't speak to your mom like that. All we're trying to say is that you can't keep bringing up comedy all the time. You can't keep doing comedy and acting like it's a job you'll get paid for." He took a sip of his coffee.

"I mean, you can tell jokes to your friends and everything, but I don't want to see you learning about comedy on YouTube or other websites. I didn't pay for devices so you could listen to random people talk about comedy. That's just stupid."

I pushed the porridge aside and lay my head down on the table in sorrow. It was officially the worst day for me.

"Do you understand that?"

And when Dad says something like that, there's no other answer I can give except, "Yes, Dad."

"Good. Now get to school."

I quickly put my leftover porridge in the sink, grabbed my backpack, and went out, slamming the door.

Okay, I know that was a little disrespectful—but my parents had just disrespected me right in front of my face by calling my comedy life stupid. Clearly, they were saying my whole life was full of stupidity.

CHAPTER 8

On that same day in school, we were handed our Math test. I guess the teacher, Mrs. Stanley, wanted us to see how bad our grades were so early, mostly because everyone looked at their test in shock and disbelief. But when I looked at mine, I wasn't shocked. Instead, I wanted to cry.

"An F?!" I got an F on my test last semester, too! Okay, I knew eventually I wouldn't pass anyway, but an F is too far! I knew that when I took this home, my parents were going to explode. They might even sign me up for that stupid school learning program.

Mrs. Stanley came up to me and frowned. "This is going on your report card, Shauna."

No! I can't believe this is happening. First, I get banned from doing comedy, and now I get an F on my Math test? What could literally get worse?

Later that afternoon, I was in the cafeteria eating my lunch when my friends came.

"Mmm, pasta and meatballs. That will taste good," Dietra said, staring at my food as she sat down.

Honestly, I wasn't really happy to talk to them.

"Hey, what's wrong?" Martin tried to make me look at him.

A minute passed, and I still didn't speak.

"C'mon, you can't ignore us forever!" Dietra said.

I sighed. "I'm not ignoring you—well, I'm not trying to, but..."

"But what?" Martin looked at me curiously.

"My parents know about the comedy club, and now they won't allow me to do comedy again."

"What?! You told them?" Dietra raised her eyebrows.

"I had to! If not, they would've made me do school learning classes. And I don't want to—but now my comedy life is ruined." I frowned and looked down. Martin put his palm over my hand, feeling bad.

"I'm sorry," he muttered.

"No, don't be," Dietra said. "Because your comedy life isn't ruined, Shauna. It isn't over yet."

"What do you mean?" I asked, looking back up.

"Your parents may force you to stop comedy jokes and stuff, but did they tell you to stop going to the club?"

"Uh... no, not really."

"Well, at least that's something—you can still do comedy there." She shrugged nonchalantly.

"But they specifically told me not to do anything with comedy in it."

"Oh, c'mon, Shauna. We know how much you want to be a comedian, and your parents can't stop you from it just like that. At least just one week in the comedy club." She sat beside me, squeezing me until I gave in.

"Oh gosh, fine! But if after that week it doesn't go well, I'm quitting the comedy club—forever."

Dietra agreed.

Although she was right, just because my parents don't like me doing comedy doesn't mean I need to quit it (unless it doesn't go well this week). And besides, they never said I should stop going to the club, so… it's worth a shot.

CHAPTER 9

After school, I went to the comedy club, and this time, I actually learned something—something that would bring my comedy belief and confidence up. "Never give up, even on the first step. It's always something you can remember when you're successful one day."

That's honestly a quote I will never forget in my life.

But after the club ended, I still went home late, around 3:30, hoping not to see Mom or Dad in the house. I sneakily went inside and quietly went up to my room.

As I was in my room writing in my journal, I got a text from the school comedy club saying,

"Hello, starter and expert comedians! I know we've just started the club in school, but this week, I've decided we should start learning how to do stand-up comedy! And so, when we learn and understand how it works, maybe we can try practicing on stage!

Please note: you don't necessarily have to do this; it's just a step that helps some people know and understand comedy more."

I can't believe it—we're finally going to do comedy on stage?!

Okay, first, I am happy about it. I've always wanted to feel what it's like to be on stage and talk about comedy. But the second thing is, how am I supposed to be on stage when my parents won't even allow me to do comedy? If they find out, they're definitely going to make me focus on those school learning classes.

The next morning, on Saturday, I was called downstairs to talk with my parents, although it was 7 a.m. and I was still sleepy.

"Ugh, what's going on? I'm still tired," I groaned while going downstairs.

"Sit down, Shauna," Mom said, looking angry.

I looked at Aaron, wondering why Mom and Dad looked furious with me. Aaron gave me a look that meant I was in trouble.

"We got some unbelievable news from the school about you," Dad said, his hands clenched on the table. "And your grades, too."

I gulped hard—now they'd definitely found out about my math test. I sat down, no longer tired, but worried.

"Aaron," Mom looked at him, "go to your room and continue your meeting. Let me know later if you got the job."

Aaron nodded and jogged upstairs, giving me a loser sign with his tongue stuck out.

"So," Dad uttered, "I don't know how or what you've been doing in school, but what I do know is... you've been failing your tests—mostly Science."

"How could that have happened?" Mom frowned. "You were doing just a bit better last semester; now you're dropping down like a fly!"

I stammered, not knowing what to say. I was actually glad they didn't ask about the math test, but I still had no excuse this time.

CHAPTER 10

"Well? Speak up!" Dad yelled.

"Look, Mom, Dad, this has nothing to do with school. I was just—my mind was just misbehaving and not thinking well in studies." I fidgeted with my hands.

"Such a lie, Shauna!" Mom said, disgruntled. "I know you, and I know exactly what's been causing this."

I looked down sadly, hoping Mom wasn't about to say what I thought she was about to say.

"That comedy thing! All this time, instead of you learning and passing in school, you're wasting your time learning about comedy and telling jokes!"

I looked up in shock. "What?! No, Mom, that's not true. I—"

"Actually, yes, your mom is right," Dad nodded.

"Anytime I pass by your room, I overhear or see you doing and talking about comedy. Never in my life have I seen you learning something like math or science."

I whined, trying to beg them. "Oh, c'mon, Mom and Dad, you know I learn! Sometimes I just don't feel like it because it won't help me in any way."

"Excuse you?!" Mom furrowed her eyebrows. "You know what? I'm done. I'm done with how you treat your life—with stupid things like comedy—instead of learning something good for your brain."

"Yeah, in fact, you're starting that school learning program," Dad added.

"What? No! You can't do that!" I raised my voice.

"Oh yes, we can," Mom said. "It's for a good cause. It's going to help you improve your school learning skills and maybe help you pass the tests you've been failing."

I started to cry. For some reason, I couldn't help it. They don't understand how horrible that class could be, and how it's not going to help me. I mean, have they ever seen my history or English tests? I always pass those! But no—my British–Irish parents only care about the *'important'* stuff: math and science.

I ran up to my room in tears and lay on my bed. But then I heard my dad yell, "Make sure you're not doing comedy but learning school topics!"

I woke up in a bad mood the next morning, just like last time, and I was sure not to talk about anything with my parents.

"Morning, Shauna, want some tea?" Mom smiled softly.

She was acting as if nothing had happened yesterday. I was still angry at them for what they did to me, so I just shook my head and sat down beside Aaron in the living room, frowning, and watched the boring sports race he was playing.

After ten minutes, Dad came downstairs, still in his pajamas, and went to the kitchen to get some Earl Grey tea.

"So," he started, "have you started learning more in your classes, Shauna?"

I groaned, becoming more annoyed.

"I'm talking to you," he said as he looked at me from the counter.

"No, but I'm going to start," I replied in a grumpy voice.

"You know, this is the best thing for you, Shauna—other than that stupid comedy thing you do. You need to set your mind on focusing on the good things, like school, trying to have a good, pleasant life—and you already know that."

At that point, I was tired of my parents and how they think I can't set my future goals without their help. Like I said, they will never understand how comedy and other good things have made my life marvelous. But this time, I wasn't going to sit down. I was going to stand up for myself. And I wasn't going to give up.

CHAPTER 11

The next week at school, I was prepared to make this day—and this week—better. Way better than last week. I had two things I had to succeed at:

1. Try to get my grades up—especially in Math, and
2. Prove to my parents that I'm not just a stupid teenager trying to tell jokes.

I'm a teenager whose mind is set on being great at what I do and becoming an accomplished comedian in the future. And getting my grades up was the first step.

So, after the last class today, I went up to Mrs. Stanley's desk to ask her something I knew I would probably fail at doing.

"Yes, Shauna?" She kept marking the test papers on the table.

"I… I'd like to ask something from you." I put my hands behind my back nervously.

"What is it?" She looked up at me.

I took a deep breath, hoping she would agree and allow me to do it. "I want to redo the math test again."

Mrs. Stanley raised her eyebrows in surprise and disbelief—even paused to understand what I was saying. And I knew why.

Mrs. Stanley was the type of teacher who would get important information from her students and keep it in mind forever. And she knew a lot about me. She knew I was already bad at Math and Science, and that I couldn't answer most questions about them. So when I asked her if I could redo the test, she already had a face full of doubt.

"Shauna," Mrs. Stanley stopped marking. "Did you just say you want to do the test again?"

"Yes. I know you're a little surprised about this, but I want to prove to my parents that I'm worthy of something. And if a higher grade on a math test is going to help, I'll do it."

Mrs. Stanley stammered a little and looked down at the papers. This time, it seemed like she was going to say no.

"Um, Shauna," she uttered. "I already started marking the tests and putting them on the report cards. I did most of them, and unfortunately... you're one of them."

I sighed, feeling a bit hurt that there was no way I could make my parents proud of me. *'I'm such a sore loser,'* my brother would say to me. And it's true—a loser is someone who's kind of dumb at things, can't win or achieve anything in life, nor can they be successful. Just like me.

"But..." Mrs. Stanley thought for a moment. "I could make an exception."

I felt hope again.

"You redo the test tomorrow, and if you pass with an 85 or above, I'll change the mark and put it on your report card."

I smiled with gladness.

"But if you fail again... unfortunately, you'll be getting an official F on your card and won't be able to get another chance."

I didn't smile when she said that, but I still had faith and hope that I would pass.

"Thank you so much, Mrs. Stanley. I won't fail you... nor will I fail this test."

Mrs. Stanley smiled, nodding and agreeing with what I said.

CHAPTER 12

I left the class still smiling, but thinking I was forgetting something.

"Oh!" Then I remembered the second thing on my *'to succeed'* list—prove my parents wrong about comedy.

I jogged downstairs to the comedy club with my backpack on my back and entered the class. I decided not to sit near the *"stinky, putrid"* girl (no offense) and instead sat in the middle row with no one beside me.

"OK," Mrs. Colleen clasped her hands together. "Glad a lot of people came today. Normally, I would barely see anyone here, but I guess it's because of the stand-up comedy practice."

I was already excited when she said that. I was ready to conquer my fear of speeches and the audience.

Mrs. Colleen started talking about what we should say to an audience and how to make it interesting for them to understand the conversation between us. And my question was—how were we supposed to be interesting? I mean, do we have to make them laugh or something?

But then she said something absurd and shocking, and it made me start to regret this decision.

"Now, FCs, you're going to start practicing by coming up here to introduce yourselves. That way, you can see and feel how the audience is going to be. After all, this class is full of twenty students—that should be enough for a big audience, right?"

She looked around the class and added, "Oh, and while you're here, at least try to be enthusiastic and tell some jokes or funny things about yourself."

She called the first person up, Koby, who was the only Black guy in the class. But while he was telling us about himself, I kept thinking about what Mrs. Colleen said.

I mean, I can tell a lot of jokes and some things about myself. But the problem is, most of my jokes—usually made up—aren't laughable. Unless it's something like the *'Britain and my dad with the Big Ben clock'* one. So are the things about myself. I don't think I could say anything funny about my jokes—or me. I guess I had to make something funny up…

After Koby and two other people went, it was my turn. I went up to the stage, which isn't really a stage, since I was just in front of the class.

Anyway, I took a deep breath, closed my eyes for a second, and said,

"Hi, I'm Shauna. And since I was a little kid, I've been interested in comedy. I always talk about it, and sometimes watch popular comedians on YouTube."

I still had no joke in my mind right then. Even though I wanted to make one up, I didn't think it would be a good one—well, maybe it would, but it might not be funny.

But then I thought of one real joke.

"And also, one thing—I told my mom I wanted to be a stand-up comedian. She said, 'Well, you'd better start by standing up to clean your room.'"

For some reason, no one laughed. I actually thought it was a good joke, though. I looked at the class and even the teacher, hoping they would at least clap. But they stared at me like they were bored with my introduction.

I gulped, feeling embarrassed. "Uh, that's... that's the end of my introduction."

That's when the class clapped and laughed. Wait... were they waiting for me to say *'the end'* before they could laugh?

Mrs. Colleen smiled at me and said, "Well done, Shauna. That was a good introduction and joke."

I went back to my seat feeling so humiliated that they didn't laugh earlier—but surprised that my introduction was actually good.

CHAPTER 13

Right after the rest of the class finished theirs, Mrs. Colleen started to tell us about stand-up comedy.

"Alright, FCs, we all know about the comedy stage performance, right? Well, anyway, I'm sure after the introductions you guys did, you have at least 50% of boldness in you to feel how an audience is. So by Wednesday, we should all be ready to go up to the stage and perform our comedy!" She clapped happily while everyone else murmured with a little excitement.

I think I had my boldness — but not just 50% of it, 100%. After class, I jumped up and down joyfully while going home. Until I reached home, it made me remember something urgent.

I entered and saw both of my parents in the living room watching the movie *Titanic*. Which is such an old movie — why would they be watching that now? I removed my shoes and went to them to say hi.

"Hi, Dad. Hi, Mom."

All of a sudden, the look on Mom and Dad's faces gave me bad vibes. I knew something was up.

"What's... going on?" I said slowly, getting closer to them.

Mom sat up straight and said, "We got some news from the school again."

"And it's about the comedy club going to do a performance," Dad said, folding his arms. Now I knew I was about to be in trouble.

"Uh…" I muttered.

"What's going on, Shauna?" Mom raised one eyebrow.

"Well, it's true. The club is going to perform on stage on Wednesday."

"And are you going to perform with them?" Dad asked. But I wasn't even scared or nervous to answer them because I was over it — over the bad treatment they always gave me.

"Uh, yeah, I am. And this time, Mom and Dad, you can't stop me, because I already signed up and said yes to the performance." I felt bold when I said that.

"Well, it wasn't like we were going to stop you, were we?" Mom said, looking at Dad.

Dad just shrugged and said, "Yeah, I don't even care about you joining school clubs and learning about comedy anymore."

He then stood up. "But what I do care about is your school learning classes. I know sometimes you learn and sometimes you don't. But I want to make a deal with you — are you in it?"

Sometimes when my parents say they're going to promise me something or make an agreement with me, they lie — all the time. So now my dad wants to make a deal with me, but I don't think it's gonna be a good one. But anyway, they're still my parents, so at no point can I say no.

"What is it?" I said, still looking boldly.

"If you do well in the comedy performance on Wednesday, we will consider you done with the school learning classes, and you can continue doing comedy for the rest of your life... without us interfering."

Now, I was actually into this deal.

"But if you fail and disappoint us on that day, you'll officially stop comedy, and I'll take all your devices away. And you will also continue with the classes and studies at school."

Mom then made a firm voice. "Was that clear?"

I gulped, hoping that everything would turn out well on performance day and that I'd finally be able to stop with the school studies. So this comedy performance was my only hope.

"Yes, I'm on the deal," I said, looking at both Mom and Dad nervously.

CHAPTER 14

That night, it was 6:40 p.m., and I was busy learning my math — not just for the test tomorrow, but also to get my math IQ level up. I knew I was so bad at math, so after studying for 15 minutes, I also went on my computer and joined the math Zoom class. I actually learned a lot from the class.

Then the time hit 7:30, and I decided to do a little comedy practice. I know my parents said no to it, but if they wanted me to please them on Wednesday, I'd have to practice.

When it was 8, I knew I had to sleep, so I quickly put my pajamas on and went to bed. As soon as I hopped on it, I closed my eyes and went to sleep like a drowsy child.

The next day was the day I was writing my test — my math test. I woke up, prayed for hope and success, and got ready for school. When I went downstairs, only Aaron was there.

"Where are Mom and Dad?" I asked, sitting down.

"They went out early this morning. Never told me where," Aaron said in an odd mood.

"What's with the face?" I asked, grabbing the leftover pancake on the table.

"Nothing." He looked at me. "But I did hear you were auditioning in a comedy club?"

"I'm not auditioning. I'm performing jokes and comedy talk in front of an audience. But you're coming, right?"

"Heck yeah! Can't wait to see my little sister perform comedy things." He rubbed my hair, making it messy.

"Okay, that's enough," I chuckled. "Let's get to school already; the bus is probably here." Then I fixed my hair, put on my shoes, and went out to the school bus with Aaron.

But unfortunately, my friends weren't on the bus, so I had to sit with Aaron in the front. I looked out the window and saw a garden in a park.

"So…" I started. "Did you know I have a math test today?"

He looked at me, confused. "What, really? I thought the 7th and 8th graders finished last month's semester tests?"

"Well, yeah, we did. But… I have to redo mine because I failed with an F."

He gave me a concerned face. "Oh, that's bad. Have Mom and Dad seen it already?"

"No, but after this test, the score is permanently going to be on my report card. So I have to pass it before they see it and start scolding me." When I said that, I felt like my hope went down — like I'd totally fail… again.

But my brother backed me up.

"Don't worry, I'm sure you'll pass." He smiled, and I turned to him. "You're a smart kid, Shauna. There's no way you can fail, not this time. And sometimes people don't succeed anyway, but they don't give up either — just like you don't in comedy. I know you don't like math, but this time, you might actually accomplish the test."

CHAPTER 15

I don't know if I should believe what he just said, because sometimes Aaron lies just to bring my hopes up. But I know when he's actually telling the truth — and as for now, he's 50% telling the truth. So I just hugged him and smiled softly.

"Thanks. Those words will definitely be in my head as I write the test."

He wrapped his arms around me like Mom does and squeezed until I coughed. "As a big brother, I can't let you fail a test like this. You can do it."

I entered the school and went to my first class, Science. Surprisingly, it wasn't so hard today. Normally, the teacher would talk about something I wouldn't understand, and I'd pay less attention because I couldn't focus well.

But not this time — I could understand the lesson better and did my work assignment with no issues.

However, things started to change when science class ended for the first break, and I had to go to Mrs. Stanley's class for the math test. Even though my brother put some hopeful words in my mind, I had a 40% bad-luck chance of passing the test. But that didn't stop me. I still went up to Mrs. Stanley's desk and saw her cleaning the board.

"Good morning, Mrs. Stanley."

She turned to me unexpectedly. "Oh, hi, Shauna! You're kind of early."

I looked at the clock — it was 9 a.m. on the dot. "Yeah, I guess I really am ready for the math test."

"Well, I expected you to come when it's lunch break so you'd have more time, but it's okay anyway." She went to her desk, grabbed the math test, and handed it to me.

"Remember the rules for tests: no speaking, no cheating, and most importantly, don't fail this time."

"Don't worry, Mrs. Stanley," I said. "I can't and won't fail this test."

She nodded and told me to sit in the front of the class. I went and sat on the nearest chair, then took out my tools for the test.

For the last time, I prayed again and started writing with confidence that I would pass. I quickly answered the questions I knew, and if I didn't know one, I just skipped it until I finished the rest — then went back to work on them. I got that idea from my mom.

Anyway, after a while, I was actually doing well on the test. What I was writing kind of made sense to me, so I knew eventually I wasn't going to fail, especially because I had studied hard for this.

When I finished, it had already taken me 13 minutes, so I gave it back to Mrs. Stanley. She looked at the test for a second, then looked at me. She did that about twice, but I didn't think it meant I failed.

"Wow, Shauna…" Mrs. Stanley started. "The test already looks good."

I smiled genuinely. "Thank you, Mrs. Stanley. I really hope it's going to be good news after you mark it."

"It surely might," she winked and smiled.

Even though we were probably just joking with each other, I really hoped the test results would be great.

CHAPTER 16

After school ended, it was time for comedy practice again. It was actually the last practice before Wednesday — which is tomorrow — when we're going to do our comedy performance.

After we practiced talking to an "audience" (which was the class) and telling jokes for about ten minutes, Mrs. Colleen had one last thing to say before the class ended.

"So," she said, and the class listened, "I know the performance is tomorrow, and we're all probably excited, but I have something to say."

She sighed. "The performance is going to have a big audience — about thirty-five or forty people are going to be there — so please be serious, and whatever you say on the show has to be… meaningful."

She then sat at her desk. "And I know it's going to be a great show, so I hope you have fun and make the comedy magic work!"

"And also," Mrs. Colleen added, "I suggest you bring your family to come watch — just for the best."

Okay, I get that my family could come. I need to show them how good I am at comedy anyway — but that's only if they like it.

The next day was another important day. It was finally time to shine — time to prove I'm right, mostly to my parents — that I'm a better comedian than they think I am.

But before I went to the comedy show, there was one last thing I had to do at the last second. Since the show was starting in about two hours, I decided to meet my friends at Prakie Park for a talk — surely about the show.

I was sitting on the bench when I saw Dietra and Martin coming my way.

I got up. "Hi, guys!"

"Hi, Shauna!" Dietra waved.

Surprisingly, I saw both of them holding hands. I was confused for a second. *Are they dating? Since when? And why didn't they tell me?*

I really didn't want to talk about it, but it kept distracting me.

"Uh, I brought you guys here to… to—"

"To what? What's the news?" Martin cut me off. But I actually didn't know why it was so frustrating to tell them.

"I'm doing a comedy show today — at school."

"Really? That's great!" Dietra exclaimed.

And I was surprised. "Yeah, I guess. But wait, aren't you guys confused, or shocked — maybe even upset I didn't tell you earlier or something?"

"No," Martin said. "Why would we be? Maybe you were busy practicing for the show or something, right?"

"Right, yeah. I was actually busy learning for a test also," I uttered.

"Why were you doing that? Our last test for this year was a week ago." Dietra tilted her head.

"Well, let's just say I didn't pass the test before, so I had to do it again. But I think I succeeded this time," I said.

"That's good, Shauna," Martin smiled.

"But…" I muttered, "what's with your hands today? Are you guys dating or something?"

They looked at each other and then at me — and quickly stopped holding hands.

"Um, yeah," Martin said. "We started dating on Monday, and it was our first go at this whole dating thing."

"It actually turned out well, too." Dietra gave Martin a heartwarming smile.

CHAPTER 17

I raised my eyebrows in shock. I never would have known my own friends would date. I mean, I did have some little feelings Martin might date earlier than me, but I wasn't thinking it would be Dietra.

Not that I hate it, but I'm just shocked. Although I'm glad he found his partner.

"You're not mad or anything, are you?" Martin rubbed his neck.

"No," I shook my head. "I'm perfectly fine with it. I hope your relationship continues to grow."

"Thanks, Shauna, you're the best," Dietra said, hugging me.

Suddenly, time passed by, and it was already noon. I had to be at the show before 12:05.

"Uh, guys, I don't think we have time to chat. I have to be at my show," I said.

"Oh, okay, we'll be there later," Dietra said.

"And don't worry," Martin touched my shoulder. "You'll do just fine. I'm sure your parents will believe in your comedy work now."

I smiled and hugged him. "I know—and I'll make sure to laugh my butt off while I prove them wrong!"

Now, I'm not sure if that was really a joke—it was quickly made up, but I'm sure it's kind of a comedy thing.

I reached the show right at 12:04, then quickly went backstage and got ready. I already saw my comedy class in front, waiting to be called. Other kids were competing too, so it wasn't just us.

I made a deal with my parents, and I know they're serious about this, so for sure they should be here—waiting and sitting in the front— to watch me do my comedy.

I already had the words and introduction I was going to say. I had two jokes, and if that's not enough, I don't know what is.

Soon, the clock on stage hit 12:10, and it was finally time to start. Two kids from my class went on stage and did their comedy, then two kids from other classes came on stage and did theirs. But then it was my turn—my turn and my time to shine.

I first walked up to Mrs. Colleen, who was holding a clipboard and standing behind the stage curtain.

"Mrs., I'm ready." I raised my shoulders with boldness.

"Alright, Shauna," she said, writing my name on the clipboard.

"Get on the stage and do your comedy magic!"

With bravery and boldness, I went onto the stage and held the microphone. Then I saw my parents, my brother, and my friends sitting in the front on the right side. I was really glad they were here, especially because my parents were smiling at me.

I took a deep breath, closed my eyes for a second, and said,

"Hi, I'm Shauna Williams, and I'm a teen who loves to talk about comedy, tell jokes, and wants to be a future comedian in life. And I'm not just being a comedian for fun, but to make people laugh and smile."

CHAPTER 18

And my quote and motivation, which I got from my comedy class, is: "Never give up, even on the first step. It's always something you can remember when you're successful one day." It inspired me to have more faith and success in comedy. And without my comedy teacher's or friends' help, I don't think I would be here."

"Anyway, now for what you've been waiting for—the jokes." I acted like I was bored and sighed. I heard little chuckles from across the auditorium.

"Math problems always say, 'If you have four pencils and take away two…' Like, no! If I had four pencils, I'd already be the richest kid in class." Laughter spread all around the left side of the room—which was mostly kids from different schools.

"I've got another one. I told my dad I want to be famous. He said, 'Well, you're already known for leaving the lights on.'" And this time, everyone in the auditorium laughed. Even my parents laughed, and they seemed to like the show. Wait—this might've worked…

The show ended, and I was getting people from the show saying, "Good job!"

"That was some great jokes!"

"And nice introduction, Shauna!"

About ten minutes later, I went to meet my family and friends by the car, and they were all pleased and happy.

"Gosh, that was an amazing show, Shauna!" Dietra clapped.

Martin came to me with a flower bouquet.

"Wow, Martin, these are my favorite flowers. Thank you!" I was so happy I made my family happy; this was my job anyway—to make people laugh and smile.

CHAPTER 19

After I finished talking to my friends, I went to my parents, hoping I had won the deal.

"So…" I started.

My mom smiled. "You did awesome up there, Shauna. I wasn't expecting it."

"Yeah, who knew my daughter was this good at comedy? And that dad joke—totally on point!" Dad added, clearly shocked.

"Mom, Dad, I was always good at something, but you kept thinking of me as a weird, unsmart kid who does stupid things. You didn't know, realize, or understand my life well. Comedy has always been in my life, even until now." I felt a relief in my heart as I said that.

"Oh my, Shauna," Mom hugged and cuddled me like a baby. "We're so sorry we didn't notice this before. If I were a good mother, then I would've supported you."

"Don't worry, Mom. No matter what choices you make for me, I will always think of you as a good mother. I understand you're just trying to do what's best for my life." I smiled as hard as I could to please them.

Suddenly, Mom got an email. She checked her phone, and it was a text from my teacher, Mrs. Stanley. Uh—oh. Was it about the test? Did I pass or did I fail?

"Oh my gosh, Shauna…" Mom covered her mouth in shock. "You passed your final semester test!"

I gasped. "Really? Yes!"

"I knew you had it in yourself, Shauna. Good job." Dad touched my shoulder.

"Does this mean I won't be doing any school learning classes?" I tilted my head, grinning happily.

"Yes, surely you won't." Dad chuckled.

I guess today was a good day. I did my math test, and I passed. I did my comedy show, and I totally proved my parents wrong. I'm so glad everything went well. Maybe I should give my story a name…

"Shauna's Stand–up."

Perfect.